Zimbabwe WomenWriters

Anthology

No. 1—English—199

Edited by Norma Kitson

Collected and presented by
Zimbabwe Women Writers
78 Kaguvi Street
Harare
Zimbabwe

Published by Zimbabwe Women Writers 1994
78 Kaguvi Street
Harare
Zimbabwe
Telephone 263 (4) 751 202

ISBN No. 0-7974-131-8-9

Cover by Inkspots Design Studios
Photographs by Wessons Photographic Specialists
Typeset by Zimbabwe Women Writers
Printed and bound in Zimbabwe
by Jongwe Printing and Publishing Co (Pvt) Ltd
PO Box 5988, Harare

Foreword by
David Karimanzira

<u>Minister of Information,</u>

<u>Posts and Telecommunications</u>

This Anthology represents three years of the selected literary work of the Zimbabwe Women Writers, an organisation which was formed in 1990.

In the 105 pieces this book contains are the thoughts, experiences and aspirations of a great number of women from all walks of life. The diversity of the material is one of its delights. The writing is from women throughout Zimbabwe, from the urban centres to the rural lands, from professional and academic women to landworkers, housewives and domestics. All of them have something important to say and I hope this book gives you as much pleasure to read as it has given me.

This 1994 English edition is to be followed by a Shona and Ndebele Anthology of ZWW selected work, and the point has to be made that the majority of the work in this present edition was written in the second and in some cases even third language of the writer. Nevertheless, the writing is of a very high standard.

Since Independence in 1980, the laws pertaining to women in Zimbabwe have been amended so that women are now equal before the Law. The contradictions between traditional and modern practice, however, mean that women are still fighting discrimination in society. A number of contributions in this volume reflect that fight.

Much of the writing is tendentious—that is also its value —and my Government welcomes the struggle of women to overcome their oppression.

More power to the elbows and pens of our Zimbabwe Women Writers!

<u>David Karimanzira</u>

still the same —
the same.
up arms and wage war.
your spear be education

Preface by
Tawona Mtshiya
National Chairperson, Zimbabwe Women Writers

I am extremely proud to present the First English Anthology of Zimbabwe Women Writers, the culmination of our work since the organisation's inception in 1990 and the work of a great number of our members.

We have presented this edition in English in order for our writers to reach a world-wide readership. This has not been an easy task. Shona and Ndebele are the mother tongues of most of our writers so that the majority of the pieces contained herein were written in the second or even third language of the writer. There are no translations in this edition. It is intended that the Shona and Ndebele Anthology will follow in 1994/1995.

The objectives of Zimbabwe Women Writers are:

1.   To promote women's writing in Zimbabwe
2.   To develop women's writing skills
3.   To encourage the reading of women's writing
4.   To promote the publication of women's writing
5.   To promote literacy among women
6.   To promote positive images of women in writing

At the beginning of 1989, a series of public discussions was held on issues concerning women's writing in Zimbabwe. This was jointly sponsored by the British Council, Alliance Francaise and the Zimbabwe/German Society. The series stimulated a great deal of debate and interest which resulted, in 1990, in a workshop in Harare for Zimbabwe women writers attended by participants from throughout the country. A small group volunteered to form a Coordinating Committee and framed a constitution to meet the formal requirements for a non-profit organisation. Since then ZWW has held numerous writing craft workshops and public readings and small selections of work have been published for our local readership.

Since its formation, ZWW has been extremely active, gaining over 500 women writers as paid-up members. We now have ZWW Branches throughout the country and the contributions covered in this book reflect work from Batsirai, Bulawayo, Chivhu, Dendenyore, Gorejena, Goromonzi, Guruve, Harare, Kushinga, Mberengwa, Railway Block, Shurugwi Urban, Tinei, Tongogara, Gwanda and Hwange.

We are greatly indebted to our sponsors: CODE, NORAD, SIDA, SAT, The Zimbabwe/German Society, The British Council and Alliance Francaise for their magnificent assistance. Thanks too, to Anne A. Knuth, Assistant Director Communication at The Ministry of Information, Posts and Telecommunications for spurring us on to publish the book ourselves and for giving so freely of her time.

Finally I would like to thank my National Executive Committee and our Branch Committees and members for their enthusiasm and hard work and to the volunteers who have always come forward to help us in our work.

I hope you enjoy reading this Anthology as much as we in ZWW have enjoyed producing it.

Please address any comments you may have to:

The Editor
Zimbabwe Women Writers
78 Kaguvi Street
PO Box 4209
Harare
Zimbabwe

Tawona Mtshiya

Contents

Contents (contd.)

Page

Contents (Contd)

Contents (Contd)   Page

Contents (Contd)

Page

1994 Zimbabwe Women Writers National Executive Committee

Head Office: 78 Kaguvi Street, Harare
Telephone (263 4) 751202

Chairperson:	Tawona Mtshiya
Vice Chair:	Doris Ndlovu
Secretary:	Mary Sandasi
Treasurer:	Valeria Chaukura
Editor:	Norma Kitson
Shona Manuscripts:	Chiedza Msengezi
Ndebele Manuscripts:	Barbara Nkala
	Rudo Mufute
	Miriam Mukiwa
	Colette Mutangadura
	Mary Tandon

& All Branch Chairpersons

Full-time Coordinator: Megan Allardice

ABOUT ZIMBABWE WOMEN WRITERS

At the beginning of 1989, a series of public discussions was held at the British Council in Harare, on issues concerning women's writing. These meetings were jointly sponsored by the British Council, Alliance Francaise and the Zimbabwe/German Society. The series stimulated a great deal of debate and interest which resulted in a workshop for Zimbabwe Women Writers in Harare one year later.

This workshop, held at the University of Zimbabwe in January 1990, and attended by over 100 women (from Harare, Chitungwiza, Bulawayo, Mutare, Marondera and other areas) was again jointly supported by the three agencies mentioned above.

Responding to the needs expressed by women writers, a large group of volunteers formed the first Coordinating Committee and, in consultation with the body of women writers, a constitution and objectives (see Chairperson's Preface) were formulated.

Since then, ZWW has been extremely active, gaining over 500 women writers as paid-up members. We circulate a quarterly Newsletter to our members, hold workshops, public readings, form small writing groups, are engaged in literacy programmes, hold seminars in women's writing for overseas universities and colleges, and are generally active in terms of our objectives.

Our membership fee is Z$5 per annum and we have a scheme whereby we ask those who can afford it to sponsor a woman writer's annual membership fee. Many rural women writers have been sponsored in this way. Women abroad who wish to obtain our Newsletters, provide sponsorship or obtain information about the organisation pay a fee of US$12.50, £10.

We now have our own office and a full-time coordinator and in May 1994 are holding a Festival—a weekend of Discussions, Workshops, Cultural Events and Public Readings.

SUPPORT ZIMBABWE WOMEN WRITERS

Vision of Motherhood

by Sheila Magadza

My vision of motherhood will always be this:

She is woken early on Sunday morning by impatient, hungry voices. Well, that's normal. The last lie-in she had was . . . um, 1976. The year her eldest started school.

The routine of breakfast, the room cluttered with discarded toys and miniature clothes. Outside, in the early sunshine, the bird chatters away in its cage and the dog grunts as it rolls over to sun its belly.

Great, she thinks, a perfect day for getting out. She announces to her three porridge-covered faces that today— for a treat—they are going somewhere.

'Where?' they demand to know.

She smiles fondly and says, 'Surprise.'

With renewed vigour, they return to their porridge.

Two hours later, having dressed them, she switches on the television and sits them in front of it as she prepares for the outing. Warm wind blows through the windows, fluttering the multicoloured curtains she has printed and sewn.

Her middle child, four years old—and already breaking hearts—keeps insisting, from her corner of the couch, that she feels sick. She ignores this and issues threats that sick people will be left behind.

Warm, yellow tangerines, apples—acid green—and sugary biscuits are popped into a plastic bag.

'OK,' she yells at the three blond heads staring with open mouths at the TV screen, 'everyone in the car.'

A burst of happy shouts, sun-hats and chubby, well-browned legs, as they gleefully hurl themselves into her battered purple car. She grits her teeth as she turns the ignition key.

'Please start,' she prays, as she pumps the gas. A splutter and then another as the car groans itself to life, making a noise similar to that of a tractor.

'Thank God!' she sighs.

Roaring through the suburbs at the fastest speed her purple comrade can muster. Sunlight streaming in the open windows and playing on the grown grass alongside the tarmac strip. Humming happily and ignoring the persistent cries from the back seat of:

'Mummy, Mummmmmyyyy . . . . my tummy is sore!'

She is unable to ignore it when a stifled scream erupts and her eldest shouts:

'Mum, she's going to be sick!'

She pulls to the side of the road and flings open the back door. As she gets out, her eldest is shouting: 'Not in the car!' while her angel-faced child is retching violently out onto the tarmac. Her youngest, a mere baby of two, watches with interest. Crisis over. Doors are slammed and the journey continues.

They arrive at the park and she is already exhausted, having stopped twice more to allow her cherub, now paler, to be sick.

'Whoopee!' the other two shout as they fall out of the car into the dusty car park.

'The Botanical Gardens!'

They amble through the park, the oldest leaping from rock to rock with monkey-like skill, the sick daughter clinging to her mother's leg for comfort.

Behind them, her son stumbles along happily on his newly-found legs.

Finding a stretch of lawn in the sun, she flops down. The day is bursting into glory like a picture book: green all around her and on her back she stares into a dazzling blue sky. Prancing around her, the children cartwheel around the lake where water lilies spread themselves out to the sun.

Her hand is tugged and she looks up to see her three blond-haired babies laughing and pleading with her to come and join them doing acrobatics on the lawn. Smiling, she does. And then she bursts into song, happily letting their mood bring the notes from her lips.

An astonished silence prevails while six round eyes above three round mouths look at her. And then her eldest says:

'Oh, Mom! Keep quiet! You're embarrassing!'

Laughing, she sings louder, until three voices are clamouring, saying: Shoosh! Yuk! Keep quiet Mum!'

The excitement is ended when the troublesome stomach throws up what remains in it. She holds the small body as it shakes in an effort to rid itself of the nasty bugs. And then a soft, sweet body nestles up sadly to hers for warmth and comfort. And she knows that even if it killed her, she would always give that comfort to them.

Their spirits dampened, the children's eyes start roving around looking for further excitement. Finding none, a voice finally says:

'This is boring. Let's go home and watch TV.'

'Yes! TV—TV—TV!' they all take up the chant.

Protesting mildly, she heaves herself off the ground and they return to their purple wagon, which faithfuly carries them home to dirty dishes, unfinished sewing, unread books, unmade beds and, of course, the TV.

<u>Untitled</u>

by Tamara Mahone

I admit I am revolutionary
but i'm taking a break to write
a love poem
if i can remember how
poem nightmares have you had one
i worry
that my lines are not
literary
enough
can you imagine
in my dreams
i was hanged for destroying the art
my poems as vehicles for advancement of a people
failed
instead use more adjectives
they said and easy
on the blackness
write about love
(it has no colour, you see, being blind)

i will re-aestheticize
myself
i will rhyme
and love

as a punishment i must write
about love

<u>Stand in the Rain</u>
(for Nelson Mandela)

by Michelle Baker

the day they set him free
i saw a man
stand in the rain
two arms raised
pumping
up and down
his fists
above his shining face
he chuckled
with the rhythm of his joy
and smiled
for freedom

Woman Writer

by Romey Buchheit

She
weathered mother
comes in from kissing
three warm sleepy cheeks

Her
huge prickly dressing gown
reminding her tired skin
to feel

Feet
icy blocks inside
discarded husband's woolly
socks

Settles
into dusty sofa with
graffiti'd clip board

Companion television
only mumbles

From the corner
ancient keys beckon
those stiff and weary
fingers

Growing Up

by Chiedza Msengezi

The bus from the Bulawayo city centre was groaning along Nketa Drive with its excessive load, when one of the passengers exclaimed, 'Look!'

All heads swung in the direction of his forefinger. There was nothing extraordinary in the view—just row upon row of new houses.

'I would have to fly a flag on the roof of mine to distinguish it from the rest—they are all identical'

His remark was greeted with a rupture of laughter. The new high density suburb of Nketa started with the erection of a few concrete, block core-houses. A core-house meant two tiny rooms: a shower-cum-toilet and a bedroom—or whatever function the owner would assign the other room. The core-houses spread, slowly at first, and then rapidly—like measles—covering hundreds of acres of land. In three months the new suburb was complete with 2,500 core-houses—units resembling uniformed soldiers all standing to attention in a smail space.

It was, indeed, difficult for the passengers—most of whom resided in the long-established suburb of Luveve—to imagine the small concrete structures as homes. Most striking was the absence of colour. The walls and asbestos roofing were a dull khaki. The ground was dusty and bare, all vegetation having been cleared to make way for the houses. On the small vacant lots left here and there as future playgrounds The grass had been burnt khaki by the long, dry summer. There was nowhere to turn eyes for relief.

For the owners, however, the core-houses symbolised a dream come true. A home at last, after fifteen years of being on the council's housing list. Spurred on by the relief, as well as the novelty of owning a house, the owners spared no effort to transform Nketa into an admirable suburb. In a few years, the major roads were lined with tall jacaranda trees in full flower, their purple canopies standing out against the blue summer sky. The small gardens were partitioned with fences, some of which were being weighed down by luxuriant bougainvillea with their purple and orange masses of flowers.

Mrs Dube, whose house stood near the main bus-stop, was most satisfied with her new home. Her colourful washing flapped on the line. Her small garden was green with leaf vegetables and fruit trees. Because her husband had planted the quick-to-grow and quick-to-fruit types, the birds were sitting in the trees eyeing the yellow pawpaws hanging like the full breasts of a nursing mother.

Inside, everything was clean, with floors so shiny you could eat off them. It seemed her family was set on the road to happiness, for it was Mrs Dube's belief that most unhappiness was caused by lack of a proper home.

Whenever her husband had stayed late at the pub or spent the night away—and the latter had happened quite often—she'd wistfully said to herself: 'What's there for a man to come home to? There's not enough space for a stool for the head of the family in this rented room.'

But her pleas to make him change these habits had fallen on deaf ears. Instead of accepting that she had failed to change him—that at 38 her husband's character was firmly set and there was no possibility of remoulding it—she kept wishing and hoping that one day he would change: that with the acquisition of a home, he would be home-bound, living happily ever after with the family.

Similarly, when her 15-year-old daughter, Selina, had brought home poor end-of-term school reports, she'd always remarked: 'It's not your fault. There is not a minute of peace and quiet for you to do your homework.'

With the new house, Mrs Dube thought her deferred hopes would be realised. In fact, she was dreaming of the day she would go to church with her husband in his best suit and announce to those church women that Selina had qualified as a doctor, after which, the women would turn to her in a gush of praise: 'What a clever and sensible girl you have raised. She should bring you home a worthy son-in-law.' To her, every dream seemed possible.

When the house was complete, Mr Dube gave Selina the biggest surprise of her life: 'Selina!' he called out from one of the bedrooms where he was positioning a newly-bought second-hand iron bed with a mattress which sagged in the middle.

Selina knelt at the doorway while her mother stood outside listening.

'This is your bedroom,' he announced.

Selina was taken aback. Even in her wildest dreams she had never thought to have her own bedroom. Her father's gesture was out of step with the normal practice in Nketa. Girls of her age slept in the kitchen or the sitting-room while rooms such as the one she had been given were rented out to bring in extra cash at the end of the month.

She babbled an effusive thanks. Her mother moved closer and added: 'You're a lucky girl. When I was your age, I never knew of such comforts—sleeping on a bed in a room of your own!'

Selina was not sure how to react to this remark. Indeed, it was not the first time she had heard her mother's woes as a poor youth. Sometimes she wondered whether her mother was happier now than she was then. However, Selina nodded in agreement.

'There is nothing to stop you from doing well at school now—go to university and study medicine,' her mother said.

9

Her father, who had a habit of making his wants and expectations known in a clear and confident tone, did not beat about the bush: 'How many girls in Nketa can boast of a bedroom of their own?' he asked.

Selina kept quiet, although her face expressed that she did not know of any.

'Yah,' he continued, 'you're not having this bedroom so you can invite our friends and fool around. I want you to get good grades at "O" level, get a well-paid, secure job. I want you to become a doctor.'

No sooner did Selina occupy her room than she developed a dislike for it. It was unbearably functional with the iron bed against the wall and a straw mat which her mother had bought from the rural women who bring their craft-work to town for sale. She tried brightening the blank white walls with pictures of pop-stars pulled out of magazines, but her mother tore them down.

'They deface my clean walls,' she said.

It was the straw mat which became the centre of Selina's dislike of her bedroom. When stepped upon, it slid this way and that over the polished cement floor. Often she hid it right under the bed, but each time her mother took it out and placed it neatly beside the bed, where it was supposed to be.

One afternoon, Selina stepped on the mat and fell. In anger, she took the mat and threw it out of the window. It landed on her mother's back while she was weeding out her bed of cabbages in the garden.

'I didn't mean to,' Selina wailed. 'I was throwing it away. I slipped on it and almost broke my leg just now.'

'Spoilt child! Plain spoilt, that is what you are. When I was your age, I had nothing to throw away.'

Selina spent the rest of the afternoon sulking and didn't do any housework.

That night Selina did not sleep well. She lay on her bed, open-eyed, her mind caught up in the night sounds. She listened to a distant train, a lone car roaring up the street, barking dogs and raised voices of drunken men returning home. The voices reminded her that her father had not yet returned from the pub, even thought it was past the pub's closing time. He'd probably gone to MaMoyo's shebeen where men congregated for a late-night drink, she thought.

Her mind shifted from the night sounds and she reflected on her parents' expectations of her.

'"O" levels—good grades—exemplary behaviour—doctor.'

The words echoed through her mind. She thought of the time before they had the house. How marvellous everything had been. Nobody expected much from her. She brought her friends home and got bad reports but nobody seemed bothered.

Now she had to pay back the bedroom by meeting her parent's huge expectations. If the recent mid-year test results were anything to go by, there wasn't a chance of her getting five 'O' levels.

'Mother can't even read and write, and father only went as far as grade seven. Not much to model myself on,' she thought as she fell asleep.

When she woke up, the mid-morning sunshine was pouring in through the lace curtains. She felt like lying in bed a little longer, even though she was breaking one of her mother's golden rules: up with the sun to work. Her mother had long been up. She had already finished cleaning the sitting-room as well as dusting her valuables—the battery clock, and collection of tea-cups in the display cabinet. She was now down on her knees with a brush and rag, ready to start on the passage floor when she noticed that Selina's door was closed. She opened it and stood hand on hip:

'Selina, you cannot lie in bed all day like a sick person! What kind of wife will you turn out to be!'

Selina looked at her mother and saw a frightful image of herself in about ten years—a life of toil and drudgery. Up with the sun to clean the house, wash the clothes, feed the famly, attend to the garden before starting

11

preparations for the next meal. She thought of the other mothers in the neighbourhood also slaving throughout the day, with babies clinging to their skirts. It was not the life she wanted. She was going to start resisting.

'What's wrong if I lie in bed for a while? A day away from school won't make any difference. I'm hopeless in class anyway. I'm not interested in learning to be an efficient housewife. And marriage isn't for me.'

Her mother was aghast at Selina's response: 'How dare you speak to me like that!' she yelled, giving Selina a long quelling stare, for which she got a long defiant one in return. She marched over and slapped Selina hard across the mouth.

Selina jumped out of bed and slapped her mother back. Then she turned and fled into the garden. Her mother was mad, yelling and screaming tearfully after her.

Mrs Dube would have liked someone to comfort her but her husband had not returned home. Was it not the worry about her husband which made her act out of character—not maintaining her usual maternal dignity? But then, she thought, even if her husband were home, she doubted it would have made a difference. He would not have known what to do with a tearful wife:

'Shut up! Stop crying like a child. It's your fault raising such an ill-mannered daughter,' was the nearest her husband had ever got to consoling her in the past.

The thought of her daughter, her own flesh and blood, slapping and shouting at her rankled and prodded her with a deep sense of injustice.

Meanwhile, Selina returned to her bedroom. She thought momentarily of suicide, but the thought vanished as quickly as it came. She wasn't brave enough for that. She decided to pack her bags and flee. That would make her mother sorry for what she had said and done. But she was not absolutely sure her mother would take the trouble to try to look for her, so that was out. Perhaps it was better just to stay at home, cold and aloof, till her mother apologised.

The next day they did not speak to or look at one another, although they stole odd glances. Sometimes, unexpectedly, their eyes met and then quickly slid past. Mrs Dube thought her daughter's atttude expressed scorn and dislike.

At night both slept badly. A couple of times Selina heard the fall of footsteps outside her bedroom and thought it was her mother coming to say it was all over—water under the bridge. This did not happen. Instead, each time the mother got as far as Selina's bedroom, her hope was dashed at the sound of the flushing toilet and the fall of more footsteps as her mother returned to her bedroom.

'Why should I apologise first,' she thought miserably. 'She started it all.'

More nights and days passed and the toll of the sleepless nights became apparent on both their faces. It occurred to Selina that she could knock on her mother's door and apologise, but she asked herself, 'Why should I'. After all, it was her mother who had started the fight.

But one evening, Selina swallowed the biggest lump of pride she had ever had and knocked on her mother's door: 'I want to say I'm sorry,' she murmured in a tremulous voice, lips pursing and twisting to keep back the tears.

Mrs Dube was relieved. But what should have been a moment of triumph for her was tarnished by the injustice of it all. The incident remained imprinted on her mind like a recurrent nightmare. She never got over it. She talked about it repeatedly to relatives who visited, always ending with the same question: 'Is it a child's place to slap her mother back?'

Things seemed back to normal. They spoke to each other and outwardly were congenial. They did their chores together and no one could have guessed the distance there was between them: Mrs Dube suffered from a deep sense of injustice and Selina felt her mother's expectations of her were unreasonable.

Would the gap ever be breached?

The Unfair Choice

by Sunungurai Mukiwa

Jennifer wiped her tears with the back of her hand and sniffed in the watery mucus from her small nose and then wiped it with the inside of the same right palm. She checked the time on her digital watch which Jabu had bought her three weeks after their first date eight months ago. She thought of the happy days when Jabu had courted her, in particular the day he turned all his pockets out to raise the ten dollars needed to buy her beautiful digital watch. Jennifer could not believe that was the same man she had talked to thirty minutes before at the City Hall. She started sobbing again and then saw two women watching her. One was so touched by her display of emotion that she nearly reached out but then hesitated and hurried out before comforting her as she had intended.

Seeing more people were coming in and out of the public toilet, Jennifer rushed to the white, enamel basin and splashed her face with cold water. She used the corner of her flared skirt to dry herself and then, putting her hands in its pockets, she went out into the bustling Bulawayo crowd. She took an emergency taxi to Luveve in Lobengula Street and then a bus home to Lupane.

The next four months were tough for Jennifer. Being a young, beautiful girl awaiting her 'O' Level results, she had never thought Jabu would let her down like this. Love, she had thought, was happiness and joy, but for her it had turned out to be just a load of pain and misery.

Fifteen years ago her parents had been killed in the crossfire when Zipra were fighting the Rhodesian Security Forces. Then UmaNcube, her aunt, had taken care of her. MaNcube had spent sleepless nights worrying about the girl's future. Now her dreams and hopes for her little niece were shattered. She had toiled hard at the market and at her old Singer sewing machine trying to make enough money for Jennifer's education. Above all she wanted Jennifer to prosper. She felt she owed this to her late brother. Now she felt betrayed and would have nothing to do with Jennifer. Her pregnancy was a disgrace and MaNcube said that by it Jennifer had proved she was a grown woman and could take care of herself. So Jennifer stayed in the house with her aunt and uncle feeling isolated and friendless.

At seven months none of Jennifer's dresses would fit. So she spent most of her time in her nightdress in the bedroom.

One morning she awoke with a sharp pain in her back and just below her tummy. She told no one and took an emergency taxi to Mpilo hospital. There, well attended by the nurses and after four hours in labour, Jennifer gave birth to a beautiful little girl.

The Samaritans visited her and gave the baby a yellow shawl, some woollies and a nightdress.

When, after a few days, Jennifer took her baby home, UmaNcube and her husband ignored her and the baby. Jennifer named her baby Muchaneta (Weakness) to show her aunt that she was being unfair. The baby grew big and strong.

Ever since she was a little girl, Jennifer dreamed of having a happy married life with a baby. She wept until her eyes were sore when she thought of her lost hopes and wished her parents were alive to share her hardship and disappointment. She thought of the harshness—the complaints and commands—she had to bear from UmaNcube. But some of the neighbours were kind and brought cast-offs from their children. Jennifer was grateful and helped them with their laundry and housework as a way of returning their kindnesses.

One morning she went to her old school to check her 'O' Level results. She had Bs in Geography, History, Accounts, Commerce and English and an A in Ndebele. She stood staring at the symbols. What use were they to her now? Her aunt would not look after her baby and so she could not further her education or get a job. The baby was an obstacle. Instead of feeling happy about her success, she felt more aggrieved.

The need to earn some money, to be free: to get back to school or to get a job, caused Jennifer many sleepless nights. Her loneliness deepened as UmaNcube's attitude towards her got colder and more hostile. She began to feel physically and mentally weak and the thought came frequently to her that in order to survive she would have to get rid of the baby. She was terrified but eventually this idea presented itself to her every day. She had no option. For survival she would have to get rid of the baby. She would have to become independent. Then her hands would start to sweat and she would feel her heart palpitating and would clutch Muchaneta close to her.

One day she read in an old magazine a story of how a woman had left her baby at the Renkini in the custody of an old woman. Perhaps she could find someone to take care of Muchaneta. She wracked her brains to try and find a solution. Who would look after her baby?

One Sunday afternoon there was a football match at Barbourfields Stadium. Jennifer decided this was her opportunity. She went to the match and handed Muchaneta to a lady who sat next to her and then went to the toilet before leaving the grounds. The plan failed because the lady followed her to the toilet. Jennifer decided to go to one of the charity organisations and leave her baby there but then got scared of her aunt's wrath. She continued thinking of ways to get rid of her baby. In her mind, she planned to return to her baby when she had a job and was settled and could afford to take care of Muchaneta.

When the baby was nine months old her aunt planned a visit to a relative in Harare. Jennifer accompanied her to the station to help with her luggage and to see her off. While waiting on the platform an idea formed in her mind. Impulsively she bought an economy class ticket to Nymandhlovu with the little money she had. Then she rushed to the 3rd and 4th platform of the main Bulawayo railway station.

The guard's voice blared out through the speakers announcing the Victoria Falls train's departure at 1900 hours. The train immediately jerked into motion amidst the farewell shouts and laughter. In the second class carriages there was confusion as passengers moved up and down trying to locate carriage numbers and compartments. Women dragged groceries in woven plastic bags. Men pulled their briefcases and suitcases with them. Pairs of schoolgirls giggled and bounced along the narrow passageway drawing attention to themselves.

After West Gate, towards Mpopoma, things began to calm down. Passengers had settled well into their allocated compartments except for a few children bumping into each other, ducking and playing in the narrow passageway.

Suddenly there was a louder shouting and swearing. Everyone tried to ignore it, thinking it was a group of drunkards. But the noise was accompanied by a small whimpering sound. Then a man, followed by four or five others, entered one compartment after another, raising his arms to reveal a baby wrapped in a yellow shawl, on which was pinned a note, asking if anyone had seen the mother of the child. People asked where the baby had been found and there was a general to-do and then the entourage would move on to the next compartment and repeat the performance. They searched carriage after carriage for the mother.

Eventually the railway officials were notified and the train was halted just before Luveve station. The police were called and were told that the baby had been picked

17

up in the toilet next to the second carriage compartment by a young man. A woman train vendor took the baby from the man and tried to comfort it. The baby, who had been whimpering now began to cry hard as people milled about. The sight of even more unfamiliar faces terrified the child.

The note pinned to the baby's shawl was little help—a desperate plea from a very desperate young woman. After the police procedures, they took the baby to Mpilo General Hospital for a medical check-up.

Jennifer read about it in the paper a few days later when she was in Masvingo having obtained a job there. She missed her baby and was still scared and weak but she clung onto the thought that what she had done was right for both her and for Muchaneta. Her baby was fit and the report said she was going to be placed in a children's home where she would be cared for.

And then, as soon as I can afford it and when I'm stronger, I'll go and claim her, thought Jennifer.

My First Step

By Norma Kitson

We were sitting in Pauline's garden in Muswell Hill one Sunday reminiscing about Durban: about how it was so hot in our home town that even if you covered yourself up all over, you'd probably still get sun-blisters; and about how handsome and powerful HA (Pauline's first husband) had been and how he had organised the sugar-cane workers in Natal. We remembered when some young visitors from India had visited Durban and there was a big party and HA disappeared into the garden with a ravishingly beautiful young girl and it was the only time in Pauline's life, she said, that she felt jealous. The young girl turned out to be Indira Gandhi and she and HA weren't smooching at all. They were talking *politics.*

Then I said wasn't it funny that David and I had lived in Gillespie Street opposite each other for most of our youth and had never met and then were introduced to each other by Rosenblatt-the-baker walking down Oxford Street in London about twenty years later.

We were having one of those nice London Sunday afternoons when you just forget the sink's full of washing up and there's all the kids clothes to wash and the house to clean plus all the other jobs you've kept putting off.

We remembered the hot-chip man who had such thin legs that, looking at him from a distance as he walked on the South Beach, it seemed he was floating a foot or two above the white powdery sand. That led us to remember the toffee-apple man, and the tall, very thin man who walked along the beach with his tray singing: "Salt peanuts

19

and toffee sweets!" and if you didn't have any money he'd give you an old stick of sugar cane from his pocket.

South Africans are very partial to sitting in their London gardens getting nostalgic about home. Well after that we sat back and made a few dirty remarks about England, and Arthur, who was still recovering from HA being so handsome, said to me:

"So what made you leave it all then?" in the tone people use when they say" "Why don't you go back to Russia?"

"What made a spoilt, rich, white girl like you get into politics, eh?"

"I don't know about spoilt," I said. "And I didn't feel rich and I don't even know if I'm white."

Arthur said: "Oh God! I'm not going to sit here and listen to you two `girls' sitting here talking about nothing. There's *work* to do. I'm going to weed the front lawn."

We all know Arthur keeps a bottle of brandy under the stone by the cherry tree.

Pauline lay back in her chair and stretched her legs out to get the sun. "Your family was dead rich", she said. "All those houses on the Berea; all those hotels; all those factories. And of course you're white. Don't be ridiculous!"

"Well," I said, "I suppose when you're young, you probably don't ever feel rich. You just accept things the way they are and that's normality to you. And if you go to Cape Town - to the Coloured cemetery there - you'll find where all the Crankos are buried. My mother used to tell us our father was "of Spanish extraction" but we all thought he was just passing for white. Then, when they wrote a biography of my cousin, John the choreographer, they said the Crankos were Huguenots or Hollanders or something *European*, because he was a friend of Princess Margaret. But you can still see them all lying buried there in the Coloured Cemetery in Cape Town. And where do you think I got my frizzy hair from?

"I want to know why you left Durban", Pauline said. "Not a whole lot of rubbish about what colour you

20

are. You look white, so you are! They'll never have you jumping up and down with pencils in your hair to see which race you are".

"Well, but there are some things you can't separate," I said. And me looking white and feeling partly black must be one of the reasons I didn't fit in at home."

"Anyway," I continued, "when I was 15 I decided to run away. I wanted to get away from my family. My mother was one of nine, so I had all those aunts, uncles and cousins. We lived within a few houses of each other on the Berea. Wherever I went, I bumped into relatives and it was worst on Fridays.

Every Friday night the whole family gathered at Grandma's house in Ridⴣe Road. We all dressed up. The men had new haircuts, wore silk hand-stitched suits and glossy ties. The women had their hair set and I had to have a comb pulled through my frizzy hair and then have it straightened with a hot-iron to get it to lie straight. It never did. We wore crepe or taffeta dresses and wedgies with your toes sticking out, and I was always being told off by one or other of my aunts because I didn't paint my nails. My Auntie Bea always spoke of my 'naked hands' as if I was running around with no broeks on.

"Don't tell me," said Pauline, "that you left Durban because your aunts wanted you to paint your nails!"

"Nails were a big thing in my family", I said to Pauline. "They sort of represented their value-system. It was bad enough if you painted them the wrong colour, but if you didn't paint them at all you were "just like a shiksa" - a real gentile outsider, you know. On Friday nights my Uncle Cyril, who became the Godfather after my Grandfather died, would choose who to see. Anyone who wanted to get engaged, or start a business, or buy a house, would have to get to speak with him. The men sat together in the `den' and the women and children in the lounge.

I think my family believed that if girls were educated, it would be hard for them to get husbands - so we all left school when we were about 14. We were supposed to take

21

a course or two in cooking or domestic science or even interior decorating but I did shorthand and typing for two terms at the Durban Business College. After that I got a job on the *Natal Daily News* in the advertisement department where I was in charge of opening the mail. I managed to extract only the adverts and discarded many of the cheques in their envelopes. I caused dreadful confusion in the accounts department and was always on the point of getting the sack.

Life was predictable. I was to hold a job of some sort for a couple of years and have a date every Saturday night - you know, get given a box of Black Magic chocolates and practise chaste kissing - and, when a boy with the right parents (and a good bank balance) came along, then, hopefully at about the age of 18 I would get married and have three or four children. To have more was considered coarse; to have less than three was a bit iffy because people might think I was frigid or that there was something wrong with my "tubes".

When a number of my cousins were going through this process, I began to dread my future.

My sister had married a dentist who suffered from asthma and the Durban humidity was very bad for him so they had been allowed to leave the family and go to Odendaalsrus. Gold had recently been discovered and there was a sudden influx of people into the tiny town and lots of work for a dentist.

I decided to run away to Odendaalsrus to be near my sister.

So one Friday night, after the endless courses of food, and when the sweet wine had been drunk and my Uncle Cyril was dealing with applications, I asked my Uncle Benny to tell him I wanted to speak with him.

"What you want?" my Uncle Benny asked. "You can tell me. He won't speak to you unless its important. You only 15. Why don't you ask Auntie Ettie?"

"Uncle Ben," I said, "I want to go to OD and stay with Joan".

Uncle Benny laughed. "Fat chance". "Hey, Cyril!",
he said, interrupting everyone, "Listen to this: *She* (pointing
at me) wants to leave Durban. My Uncle Cyril laughed.
"You go in the lounge with the girls, darling," he said. And
Uncle Benny gave me a fond smack on the bum, dismissing
me.

I had to run away. They wouldn't even listen. I had
some money saved up from my wages and I bought a train
ticket to Odendaalsrus and spent the next couple of weeks
hinting broadly that I wanted to leave Durban. But no one
took me seriously. So I left a note propped on my father's
dresser, another on my mother's bedside table and I also
told everyone in the kitchen I was going to Joan in
Odendaalsrus.

"Hau! Miss Norma", said Joseph the cook.

It was a depressing thing to hear. It expressed the
total horror of what I was about to do - the impossibility of
it all.

But I cabled Joan and, as everyone was out except
our Nurse McGrath, I told her I was going to spend the
evening with my cousin Wendy, took a small overnight
case and walked to the Durban station. I caught the night
train. I had an uncomfortable journey, wondering if the
police would haul me off at the next station or if irate junior
Uncles speeding in Oldsmobiles would arrive to fetch me
home. But I arrived without incident and Joan gave me a
warm and wonderful welcome. Durban was behind me.
The arguments, the objections, the tears and entreaties
were all to be dealt with from a distance and from Joan's
protective custody.

My sister was warm and welcoming. She was wide-
eyed and excited that I had struck out on my own and
defied the family. She and Rolf were living in a small room
behind the surgery, so I would have to get a job - the Mine
was the only possibility - and a place to stay.

They were shaft-sinking at Freddies South and I
applied for the position of Secretary to the Study
Department. At my interview I was asked whether I could

type a stencil and whether I could read a graph; whether I could work a switchboard and a duplicator. I said yes to everything. If I admitted there was anything I could not do, I felt sure I wouldn't get the job.

I arrived at the Mine office with my face covered in Leichner make-up, hair slicked down and wearing wedgie shoes, hoping to look as old as 18. But it didn't matter. There were few women to fill the many office jobs and I was welcomed, taken on immediately, and asked to relieve the telephonist at lunch time.

The switchboard turned out to be a little glassed-in room banked by three metal walls containing numerous small black squares. Each square had a hole like a hooded eye and convex grey discs with numbers flicked up and down over them, each making its own clicking noise. In some of the holes were strange-looking plugs with thick black cords which criss-crossed each other and made a mess of the whole panorama of technology.

As soon as I entered the room, the operator, Yvette, indicated a notepad with a list of names, grabbed her bag and left, saying: "See you?".

I sat down with the three walls of grey discs clicking at me and a row of things buzzing in front of me. I decided to start from the beginning. I had to stop all the clicks and buzzes so I could concentrate and work the thing out. I opened my arms wide and gathered the cords in both hands and, sweeping them into a holdable mass, yanked them out of their holes. The clicks became more insistent and people began tapping on the glass door of the switchboard room, so I got up and opened the door a fraction. "What you want?" I was trembling and nearly sobbing with terror.

"I was cut off!"

"I was talking to the Underground Manager of Freddies North and I was cut off!"

"Something went wrong with my phone. For God's sake! Get that call back right now?"

I said to everyone: "The switchboard's out of order

24

and the engineer is busy fixing it now. I'll get your call back as soon as he's through.

I went on saying things like that through the lunch hour. When Yvette came back from lunch she took one look at the board - all the silver plug heads neatly in their front slots, cords out of sight, the board silent except for a few clicks here and there - and she said: "You've never used a switchboard in your life, have you?"

"Well, no, not one like this", I said.

She laughed and stayed with me for a few days during her lunch hours until I learned all about switchboards.

The Mine was new and my office was luxurious, with a large desk, new Remington typewriter, couch and easy chairs, wall cabinets and bookshelves and a pile carpet. I went through the drawers of the desk and among the rubbers, paper clips and biros, discovered three bottles of red nail polish which I immediately threw in the bin.

The Remington typewriter was new to me. Babette, in Geology, taught me how to switch the machine to *stencil* to disengage the ribbon and enable the type bars to cut through the wax. These were terrifying days for typists - before Tipp-Ex - and I found that if I made a typing error on a stencil there was no way to rub it out. You had to have *perfect* typing! It sometimes took me 8 stencils to get a perfect original.

On the Thursday of my second week at the job, I returned from my relief stint on the switchboard, and my boss, a very polite Swiss, Mr Sahli, called me into his office.

"I see you've requisitioned for another box of stencils, Miss Cranko," he said.

"Yes, we do use an awful lot of them."

"I've noticed", he said. "But we had a three-month supply in, you know."

A couple of days later he came into my office with an armful of stencils he had extracted from my waste-paper basket. "Haven't you heard of correcting fluid, Miss Cranko?"

Oh, the terror of those days!

I requisitioned immediately for 'correcting fluid' from Stationery and the next day there arrived on my desk three bottles of the red stuff I had thought was nail polish.

I learned the hard way - like most people do. I was confronted with the fact that I had lied about my age, that I couldn't read graphs or work a Roneo machine, but everyone was very kind.

Twice a week I went down the Mine with my boss and representatives from all the sections that were responsible to the Study Department. It was a terrifying journey in a Mary Ann—a bucket —that swayed and bumped its way down two terrifying miles. Freddies South is one of the deepest mines in the world and of course there are no lifts during shaft sinking.

I was given a small room in a house in the married quarters with a young Afrikaans couple, Suzette and Fanie de Jongh. Suzette was a wonderful cook and housewife. I learned a lot from her and ate some of the best meals in my life there and I was very happy. Fanie was a shiftboss at Freddies. He had a magnetic personality and the couple was very popular. They always had visitors and there were endless relays of tea, beer and *koeksusters.*

Fanie was a great raconteur and told fantastic tales: of underground, of the dangers of working two miles from the surface, of heat exhaustion and the hazard of methane gas, of the shortage of labour and the Mine recruitment programmes for black workers. He told us stories of camping out in the veld, of dangerous animals, no water, getting lost in the bush and, finally, without food, finding the way home again.

He told us, in the rhythmical way Afrikaners have, the story of how they first arrived in Odendaalsrus, when Suzette was 6 months pregnant and there was no accommodation at all and how they had to live in their Dodge— "Kitchen in the bloody boot, bedroom in the back. Radio, the lot, Man! I used to shave with the radiator water, but it was worth it boy-o. Talk about rags to riches! That's the understatement of the bloody millenium, you know, It was unreal, you know. There's nothing so marvellous as shaft sinking money with added danger money and shift pay and on top of that, overtime. Out a'sight, man!"

I loved Fanie's stories, always told with explosive enthusiasm. Everyone would agree with him, however outlandish his views and anecdotes would follow about how this one had left a lousy-paid job on the Rand or Rustenburg to get shaft sinking pay and what a difference it had made to their lives. Or how it was difficult to know where the best jobs were: Odendaalsrus or Welkom - a town a little way away where gold had also just been discovered and the Welkom Mine was starting.

There were also endless stories about the 'foreigners' - the Swiss, English and German mining engineers who formed a quite separate social group.

"He might well be a bloody good engineer but he knows nothing about kaffirs and boerewors," I remember him saying. "He speaks to kaffirs as if they was white and he says boerewors makes him vomit. God, man, hy's 'n rerige bliksemse rooinek!" (God man, he's a real English git).

I was embarrassed when the Jews were the subject of their swearing, but they seemed not to notice my presence. "Bliksemse Jode! Its a pity Hitler didn't finish the whole bloody lot off, man."

One Sunday, about twenty of the de Jongh's friends came to a braaivleis. We sat in the garden - a new bare patch of red earth—on striped beach chairs. The beer flowed and the marinaded steak and boerewors sizzled on the braai. And Fanie told a story that changed my life:

The white miners were given lectures on the dangers of smoking underground because of the presence of methane gas. It was clear that these talks made little impression on the white shift bosses. But the black miners were shown horror films of the results of naked flames. These were terrible constructions of explosions, with bodies blown apart and blood and guts spattered on the rocks underground. The dangers were very real. There were accidents—explosions and fatalities—every day during shaft-sinking at Freddies. No black miner could have escaped seeing a colleague either killed or injured by a rock-fall and losing a limb was a daily hazard. The miners wore Edison Safety Cap Lamps to detect methane and the black miners were very conscious of the danger of a naked flame undergound.

On this afternoon, amidst the roasting braai and salads, the hot sun and warm people, the iced beer and the warm peaches, Fanie was sitting in his shorts, leaning forward in his seat, telling this story:

"I was down there. It was about three hours after the shift began and I was dying for a smoke. I left the boys to get on with it and took myself off by the rocks and lit up. Bugger me if the Boss Boy - that Sam - doesn't come up to me:

"Basie", he says to me, "Basie, the gang asked me to come and have a word with you, please baas."

"Don't stand there looking half-cocked," I said. "What d'you want?"

He was rubbing his hands and I could see he was damn scared.

"Please Basie, don't smoke down here. It's too dangerous. They sent me to ask you. Please Baas. There's methane here!"

"I looked at him. I tell you I was bloody angry. I was fucking annoyed."

"Bloody kaffir! Who are you to tell me what to do? OK, OK you say its all the boys. OK you boys, now who else thinks that he can tell me what to do here, hey? Who else feels he wants to criticise me as if I don't know what I'm doing? Ja, just you come forward, man."

"Three of the buggers steps up to me. And then," Fanie said to us, enjoying the denouement of his story and the exercise of his power, "And then I said, `OK you boys.

28

Each of you take the end of a vent pipe now, and take it up to Level Two and back here again, OK?".'

He made the four men carry two heavy vent pipes up and down from level to level until they collapsed from fatigue and heat exhaustion. Then they were sent to the surface where an ambulance took them off to hospital.

"I was so bloody angry, I can tell you. I was so fokin' annoyed I didn't give them their salt tablets. But one thing's for sure. I won't have that lot breathing down my neck again. That'll teach the buggers to question my authority, isn't it? I'll tell you, I won't have no more trouble out of that bloody gang. Jesus, man! They'll just have to get me another Bossboy. If you get a bad one on your team, you've had it, you know?"

To a chorus of 'cheeky bloody kaffirs!' and 'Jesus, man, you should of given him a bladdy good hiding first!' I left the room.

I packed my case, went to Joan to say goodbye, and caught the train to Johannesburg that night.

The next day I joined The African National Congress.

I glanced over at Pauline and saw that she was nearly asleep.

Arthur staggered towards us, stepping right into her newly-planted seedbeds.

"You'll catch it!" I whispered.

He gave me a tipsy look and then lay down on his back on the grass.

Comfortable, I thought. They're all so comfortable in England.

There are no ladies here

by Hilary Homans

(Written on the evening of Wednesday 2nd May 1990 immediately following a ZIWU meeting)

The 'gentleman' announced:
'Now we'd like to hear from the ladies.
The front row is reserved for the ladies.'
He didn't mean to be unkind, insulting.
Perhaps he was trying to encourage us.
Maybe he genuinely wanted to hear what we have to
    say.
But, there are no ladies here!

Doesn't he know that the term 'lady' means
'Mistress of the house'?
Are there any mistresses here?
Are there any women attached to houses here?

'Lady' also implies
'Female of rank'—of royal blood.
Are there any princesses here?
Any Lady Diana's? Any MaiMugabe's?

There are women though—
'Human beings of the female sex'
'Adult human females'
We are here.

But we had our say last week
At the Women's Writers Readings.
Maybe tonight we are tired.
Maybe tonight we want to listen to what
The great man of distinction has to say
(But I doubt it . . .)

Last week was different though.
We were not silent then.
In a room so full that it was difficult to move, to
    breathe
In a room so full of energy, excitement, and for some
    of us emotion,
Where we heard the women's voices—
We had our say then.

Be reassured:
We will speak here
In our own time,
When we have something to say.
In the meantime, though,
There are no ladies here.

Makhoza

by Luness Mhlope

They used to swear by her name.
They used to swallow by her name

    MAKHOZA!

Mother of the young
Mother of the old
The pounded rapoko
Will stay fresh—
Don't throw it away!

    IS SHE?

Makhoza! Makhoza!
Oh! Let it not be said
You are dead!

The Beginning of a Novel

(From the ZWW June 1990 Workshop)

by Julie Frederikse

Sara looked down at the stream of milk pouring out of the cracked baby cup onto the kitchen floor and her eyes moved from the spreading white puddle up her leg, taking in the wet splotches on her trousers. One of the many freedoms she had felt when she finally stopped breastfeeding Kimon at the age of two years and three months—aside from the relief at the end of the stares and comments from strangers: 'Dedicated mother, you, but isn't he a bit old now?'—was in celebrating an end to the inescapable smell of souring milk. But even after the doctors had decided that Kimon was ready to drink cow's milk and not hers, from a cup and not from her grotesquely heavy breasts, she still couldn't seem to escape the smell of milk—usually spilled from a hurled cup.

Those cute little cups with the grinning bear on the side advertised as untippable—by any normal child. She'd winced when the saleswoman said that: 'Marvellous invention—no normal child could possibly manage to tip it over!'

But Sara was not the mother of any normal child.

She had never thought before that a word could torment a person so. She and her brother had used that word as a kind of joke between them when they were growing up: 'Mrs Simmonds is coming to supper, so please try to act normal—*try*!' And Tony would cross his eyes and roll his head, and they would both burst into laughter.

Whenever she and Tony got together, after they had grown up and left home, they would always manage to work in that joke. If they had been out drinking, for instance, Tony would slink up and whisper in her ear, 'Just try and act *normal* and everything will be okay.' He got extra mileage out of the joke when she was pregnant, doing imitations of her waddling along, saying, 'I know it's hard to act normal, but please try!'

Those jokes had stopped when Kimon was born. 'Normal' was so obviously what Kimon was *not* that people made sure they made no reference to either normality or abnormality when Sara was around.

'Mrs Sanderson,' the doctor began as she sat in the post-delivery room several hours after that interminable day of fear and pain that had finally ended with Kimon's birth. She thought at first that they were just giving her time to recover from the ordeal, and would bring that screeching reddish bundle to her at any moment and put him to her breast. But as the time wore ón, and the nurses told her to 'just wait for the doctor' when she asked where her baby was, she knew that there was something terribly wrong.

That was when the word 'normal' first entered her head without the warm and funny connotations of Tony's jokes. 'It's not normal,' she kept saying over and over to herself. When the masked doctor pulled back the faded flowered curtain around her bed and removed the white curtain in front of his mouth to reveal a surprising red moustache and bad teeth, she wanted to do as the nurses did and put a finger to her lips to indicate silence. 'I don't want to hear it,' she felt like telling him, and then ordering him out of her curtained space.

'I don't want to hear that word.' Because Sara knew this doctor wasn't going to use it the way Aunt Ellen had when she had rung up to excitedly report the birth of her grandchild. 'It was a terribly long labour and they were really worried toward the end, but thank God the baby's normal.' Sara remembered how her friend, Pat, had announced the premature birth of her son: 'Tiny, but with ten fingers and ten toes—perfectly normal.'

She knew the doctor was going to tell her that this baby she had carried for eight months and three-and-a-half weeks was *not* normal. She knew that the fear that had dogged her throughout those long months was now a reality. She had given birth to a monster-child.

Sara looked down again at the puddle of milk at her feet, and at the untippable cup wedged between the table leg and the wall. She picked up a dishcloth, daubed uselessly at her damp pants, and looked into Kimon's half-closed eyes as she thought back to the day he was born. She recalled the dread she had felt rising through her body when the red-moustached doctor had gravely begun his report on her then still unnamed and unseen child. She hadn't even known for sure then that he was a boy, although she thought she had heard a nurse whisper that 'he's under observation'. All that Sara knew for sure, as the doctor groped for words, was that she was about to be told that her baby was not normal.

Singing the Blues

by Pat Made

Seems like the last nine years
of my life I've been
singing the blues

Crying inside for a better future
crying inside for all I want to be

Singing the blues comes easy to me
because it seems like such a crime
to be happy

Maybe all my life
I've been singing the blues
and just hadn't realised
how easy it had become

I like singing the blues
'cause it keeps me in chains

I like singing the blues
'cause I don't have to face tomorrow

Freedom

(From the June 1990 Workshop)

by Beryl Aschmann

After the policeman left, she sank wearily onto the lumpy, over-stuffed sofa—which served as both chair and bed—and wept. Some time later, all her tears spent, she raised her head from her hands, looked round and mentally began to take stock of her situation. Her eyes travelled slowly around the darkening room, noting the plaster peeling from the walls just below the ceiling, the poky fireplace with its blackened hearth, the lifting floorboards, tattered curtains at the windows, shabby chair in the corner and, finally, the front door hanging lopsided from its hinges.

Freedom. Just on the other side of that door was freedom.

She gave a deep, trembling sigh and her hand moved slowly towards her neck as she felt for the chain that had become so much a part of her during the last few weeks.

'Don't lose it,' he had said to her that night, 'and whatever happens, don't let anyone take it from you.'

That night. Was it really only three weeks ago? She sighed again.

'Well, at least they didn't take it from me,' she

thought, a cynical smile tilting the corners of her mouth. 'I've kept that part of the bargain so far.'

She lifted the chain from inside her collar and held in her hand a small key.

'Freedom,' she said aloud. 'Is this my key to freedom?'

Again her eyes travelled to the front door. Her nostrils flared as she drew breath sharply inward. Her heart was thudding against her chest. She felt the overwhelming waves of fear sweep over her again. Would she ever be free? Was it really her destiny to be imprisoned in this cage of fear forever?

'Maria Coles,' she chided herself, 'You know very well that the only key to your prison is courage, and that you hold that key.'

She took a deep breath, rose to her feet and very quicky walked over to the tatty archair in the corner. From behind it she pulled a well-used but expensive leather suitcase which she heaved on to the lumpy sofa. She was moving very decisively now, almost mechanically. Swiftly opening the suitcase, she strode across the room to the old chest of drawers and began transferring her clothes into the suitcase, which was only half full when she banged the lid closed.

Maria cast one more fleeting glance around the room, picked up the suitcase and without another moment's hesitation, ran out of the lopsided front door.

Djoniba's Drum

♪ ♪ ♫ ♪

by Jennifer Ann Sharpe

Palms plunge and aim
to meet the heart. . .
(Base resounds)

Closed fingers pat the rim . . .
(Middle sounds)

Hands bases whip edges,
tips lash forth, then hover . . .
(High notes)

Now beat the drum
don't burst its tight-bound skin.
The dancers, taut,
are ready to begin

Leaps—Twirls—Falls.

Segments—Cadences . . .
Rivulets of sweat.

Calabashes whirl,
rattling their beads . . .

Beating hand bloodied
bound quickly by rag,
rhythm undaunted.

The African Woman

by Maria Kaz Mushava

He always greeted her with a gruff: 'Hello'.

In his voice was neither contempt nor appreciation. He was simply indifferent. He would enter, sit in his soft armchair, and slam the door shut with the back of his left hand. He would rub his eyes, sneeze—or should I say bellow. Then, he would remove his sweat-filled shoes—Pino Gardini (he had style), right there, in the middle of the lounge.

Next, he would start peeling off his socks, with one hand, while the other reached for his Coke and Brandy. Half his sentence would be lost in the large mug, yet he'd look up, clearly irritated by her lack of response. Quietly and patiently, she'd ask him what it was he'd been asking, and he'd click his tongue at her impatiently and repeat loudly: 'I said, what did *you* do with yourself today?'

This was what he'd become as the years rolled—or should I say—rumbled, by. Impatient irritable and restless.

Amai Sharon would have usually looked at him through her small black eyes, and answered: 'Oh, I knitted as usual.'

But not today. Today she would tell him the truth. She was tired of being submissive. She was tired of talking to a brick wall. When she opened her mouth today, she was going to be honest. For too long she'd let him walk all over her. For too long he had had his own way and never asked her how she felt. For too long she had danced to whatever tune he played.

She wrung her hands in inner agony. The tears rolled slowly down her gaunt-looking face and she felt as if one hundred African drums were beating incessantly in her head.

The telephone rang. She jumped up in fear. Baba vaSharon might be hurt. For ten years she'd been afraid of the phone. It was the vessel that delivered news of him. Baba vaSharon was a fireman. It frightened her to think that this time it might not be his gruff voice on the other side.

No! No! No! she told herself. Today I shall be calm when I pick up the phone. After all, it might be that woman he was having an affair with who, feeling equally insecure, found it necessary regularly to instil fear of desertion in Amai Sharon.

'Hello?' she said calmly.

'Are you there, Amai Sharon? I just thought I'd tell you he's done it again. I'm sorry, I know how it feels, and I felt the least I could do was to let you know before he got home. I'm sorry Amai Sharon!'

She rang off before Amai Sharon could reply. Not that she ever replied when this sort of phone call came in. What could she say? What on this earth could she possibly say that would alter things? Nothing! She could do nothing to him after all he had said and done.

But not today! That had been the last time. She would never have to cry again. She would never have to use her three children as a reason for staying married to Baba vaSharon. Never again would she belittle herself just to make him feel like a king in his own palace! Never!

VaMyoyo, his mother, was a good woman. She was a hard woman, but she was a good woman. Every time another of Baba vaSharon's girlfriends fell pregnant, VaMyoyo would break the news gently to Amai Sharon. But then, pain is pain. Humiliation is humiliation. It doesn't matter who inficts it. Its scars are always deep and inerasable.

At first, that is, during the first two years of her marriage, Amai Sharon had thought maybe it was her fault. She had changed her Afro hairstyle and had had a perm. Secondly, she had bought shorter skirts and tighter blouses. After being almost brainwashed by a so-called 'friend', she'd even contemplated

41

seeing the Herbalist who lived in Seke.

But no! He hadn't changed. Not one little bit. Gone was the laughter. She was no longer treated like a newly laid egg. She was now a nobody. Sometimes she wondered what he said to his friends at work when they asked about the children and his wife. I bet, she mused, he says: 'Oh Amai Sharon and the family couldn't be better. I'm giving them all I've got.'

You see, that's how he saw them. As his duty—and nothing else. He was a provider. That's all.

Amai Sharon remembered an incident a few years before, when she'd pointed out that he'd bought her the same dress twice in a row. He'd looked up from his newspaper, clearly perplexed, and said:

'So what are you going to do about it? Throw them all away? Do I have to tell you to buy some new materials and buttons to add to each dress to make them look different?'

With that, he'd clicked his tongue at her in irritation before returning to the paper. Since then, she'd chosen to suffer silently instead of speaking up.

But not today! Enough was enough. She had gone to the employment agency in town, and had shown them her Diploma in Interior Decorating. This time, she was going to live for herself. She would buy all the things she'd always craved. After today, she'd be a new woman. She would not play second fiddle to anyone, least of all to a man. She had a way out. She had previously lacked the courage but knowing that a fifth child of Baba vaSharon's was about to be born, as VaMyoyo had said, was the last straw! He'd been unfaithful before. It was not the first time, obviously, but she'd finally realised that he wasn't going to change his lifestyle for her (yes, that's what he called it—a lifestyle!). She certainly wasn't going to be his doormat! She wasn't doing it for revenge. No! An eye for an eye and a tooth for a tooth, certainly wasn't the issue. She just wanted to be somebody. Not for him or her children.

'No,' she thought. 'For ME. Just for me.'

The house shook as Baba vaSharon entered. As usual he greeted her with a gruff: 'Hello'.

In his voice was neither contempt nor appreciation. He

42

was, as usual, simply indifferent. He slammed the door shut with the back of his left hand. He sat in his armchair. He rubbed his eyes, bellowed, then took off his sweat-filled shoes—right there in the lounge where Amai Sharon was sitting, looking at him, her eyes sparkling with determination.

As usual, half his sentence was lost in his mug which contained Coke and Brandy—of which he was partaking—whilst he peeled off those sweat-filled socks of his. For once, she did not ask him what it was he'd been asking. She simply stared at her husband, who was as alien as an alien could be.

So used to being asked, it was quite a while before he realised he'd bellowed out his answer to the woman who sat holding his newspaper quite clamly. She usually jumped up and answered him patiently and meekly. He drained the contents of the mug, as if suddenly needing the drink to give him Dutch courage—rather pointless if one lives in Zimbabwe!

Amai Sharon slowly put the newspaper down. She looked squarely at him, then said: 'I gather you've had a usual day. That is, of course, a day filled with complaints from the mothers of four different children, each a few days and, in some cases, even hours, younger than the last. I also know that you'll soon have a full basketball team one of these fine days. That's all right by me. After all, it's your money, not ours, as I'd foolishly believed.

'Now let me tell you something. I got a job today. It appears I'm not half as worthless as you've made me feel for ten years! There are actually people out there who respect me, who talk—not bellow—at me, who listen when I open my mouth—not push the paper in my face. I also learned that I can be so many things. Now that there will be two breadwinners in this family, things are going to change around here—or someone is going to have to move out. And that someone is not ME!

'I shall not sit up at night wondering where you are or who you are with. I'm going to sleep all night, and I will snore if necessary. Now, if I have managed to live with you for ten years, and have never questioned your whereabouts, let's see if you can do the same. From now on, I'm going to be just ME!'

He stared.

Every Woman who writes is a Survivor

by Amanda Hammar

(I)   bleed
and the blood red earth
is your mirror

weep
and the soil erodes
with your sorrow

write
and the ground beneath you
grows fertile
with hope

(II)   she has written
and she says
it moved her

it pierced
a forsaken place
with sharp words
searchlighting
gargantuan pain

(III)   cut open the words
spill the juices
of your hidden longings

Special Clearance

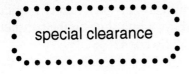

by Fiona Lloyd

'Special Clearance'—the words stand out, livid and purple on my pale forearm. I am branded, marked. The others in the queue offer their palms. 'Special Clearance'? Perhaps the Manager's brother runs a wholesale chain—one of those barn-like places with bolts of java print and an Indian cashier who still serves the white housewives first. Andy will like the stamp, though. He will talk about hidden codes and semiotic meanings.

I hope he's here.

It's cold. The stars are shards of broken glass, littering a vacant sky. Somewhere, far off, a train whistle despairs. In the townships there are the shebeens and the beerhalls: in the Northern Suburbs the Bridge parties and the South African wine, but here only a centre which has no centre.

He said he'd be outside. He isn't. Its 1.30 and I'm not hanging around by myself. I'm not going home, either. I've been stamped.

Inside there's this tunnel with red carpet up the wall. It smells of beer and sweat. And then the music and the dancers: jerking puppets under the strobe lights and the peeling posters of Michael Jackson. It's trying so hard, the Playboy Nightclub. Like a child dressed up in grownup's clothes. It totters on shoes that are five sizes too big. It is not New York and it is not London and I am as safe as I have always been in this city which is no city.

'Where are you from? Are you from Germany?'

'What?'

'You're German. So, how's Zimbabwe?' He has his arms round my shoulders. I ease towards a carpeted pillar.

'I'm not German. I'm waiting for my boyfriend.' I sound ridiculous. He grins, tapping a shiny white shoe on the parquet.

'So. Where are you from? Sweden?'

He leans towards me, smiling, friendly.'What's the matter? Are you afraid of black men?'

He says it softly like a secret into my ear. And then he smiles again and is gone. He thought I was a foreigner. 'Are you afraid of black men? Oh, yes. I bet that one works really well with the Germans and the Swedes. I feel like shouting across the dance floor: 'I'm a Zimbabwean! I'm as Zimbabwean as you are!' But I don't.

A hand tugs at my dress. 'Sit.'

I noticed her when I came in and wondered how old she was—fourteen, fifteen maybe. Wearing a stained white dress with shoulder straps that she keeps hitching up.

'Sit down.'

She wriggles to make space for me, leaving a sweat mark on the plastic sofa. 'Cigarette?'

'No thanks—I don't smoke.'

'No man, I mean have you *got* one? Hell, never mind.' She grins and I know she is not fourteen or fifteen. A thin bird of a woman with unwashed hair and nails that are painted lovingly, exquisitely. She jerks her head towards the pillar where I was standing.

'Men,' she says. 'Sometimes you have to tell them exactly where they gets off. Even . . .' she leans towards me, '. . . even if you has to use a bit of *language*. Know what I mean? I don't have to take crap from them. I tell them—first sign of crap—I tell them, "Fuck off!" That's what I say.'

There is a man in a suit sitting opposite us. He glances up and catches her eye.

'Fuck off!' she shouts, happily, affectionately, almost. He does.

So we sit on the tacky sofa drinking Castle. Her name is Ruby. Ruby Zolto. She was married to a Hungarian for nine years. She has four children—three girls and a little boy who's only four. He'll look after his sisters when Ruby is six feet under.

'Hell, they beautiful,' she tells me. 'People look at them and say, "Ruby, how they *yours*?" They got blue eyes and they *beautiful*. If you saw them you'd think I was looking after a white couple's kids. Really!.'

I do not look at her. Where is Andy?

'Hey! You married?'

'No. I have a boyfriend, though.'

'Is it? Is he . . . OK?'

'Yes, he's nice.' A lame answer. Andy's more than nice. But what does she mean?

'That's good. I'm glad he's nice. Is he also white?'

'Yes.' And something makes me add: 'He's Zimbabwean, like me.'

'Oh.'

Ruby grips my wrist. Strongly. Laughs. 'I thought you was foreign, you know?'

'I'm not. I've lived here all my life.'

'Shit! It's a hole, hey? Harare. I'm not really from here, you know. Well, my Dad's from Bulawayo. But my Ma—she was born in Port Elizabeth. So I'm half South African, really. And I was married to this Hungarian.'

We drink our beer. The music seems far away.

'I had a white boyfriend once,' says Ruby. 'I mean a real boyfriend—I didn't do it for money with him. Hell, he was handsome. As handsome as a bastard. As handome as Prince Charles. No! Handsomer. He used to come to my place in Arcadia in the night and go again before morning. And then he left.'

The music is suddenly slower—some sweet, sad song by Tracey Chapman. The dance floor empties. Ruby holds my wrist again like a woman who is drowning.

'This is *my* song!' she whispers. 'This is about me . . . come!'

And we are almost the only people dancing. People stare as Ruby closes her eyes and sways to the story of love and betrayal. And then it's over and the place pulsates again to

Zairean rhumba. Ruby wrinkles up her face.

'Af music!' she shouts. 'Let's sit!'

So we sit and drink more Castle and my hair feels stiff with cigarette smoke. Ruby darts off. 'I'm back just now!' she shouts.

I don't feel so safe without her—too many eyes, too many unspoken demands and challenges. But soon she returns with a bit of paper torn from a margin of the *Herald*. She has written something on it with her eyebrow pencil: 'Ruby Zolto, 119 Cloverleaf Flats, Arcadia.'

'There! Now you can come and visit.'

She says it carelessly, leans over to do up her sandal. When I was a child, I remember, I used to write my name and address on a balloon and send it up over the treetops. Nobody ever found it. Or if they did they never wrote back.

When I turn round Ruby has gone. The sofa carries the mark from her bare back. As I watch the sweat disappears into the plastic.

Andy never did come—something about a late meeting and feeling tired. On Monday when I saw him at the office he didn't notice the faint mark on my forearm. 'Special Clearance' it still said. It had turned the colour of a bruise.

Short Story

by Romey Buchheit

I'll never forget the first time I heard your name. It floated off his lips, did a gentle flick-flack in space, quietly catapulted off the walls, and hung—over his head—like a halo.

'Who is she?' I asked.

'A friend,' he answered. 'An anthroposophist. She lives in England.'

'Oh,' I said, suddenly feeling so insignificant. I was an almost ex-lover, a mother, living in Zimbabwe.

The next time I heard your name, it flew off his lips, hurtled straight across the room and hit me in the gut-plexus.

'She's moving in tomorrow,' he added. This time I said more than just, 'Oh!'

I rushed home and attacked the typewriter. Five-and-a-half years of confused anger raged onto the paper. I had tried to say it all before, of course, in so many different ways, but it never seemed to come out right. But writing it down—that really worked. I made a copy for you, put it carefully into an envelope and delivered it to you personally early the next morning. My hand shook as I rang the bell. The door opened and there you stood.

'I'm the father—I mean, you're the mother, no, you're the father—' I blurted out. Then I got it right. 'I'm the mother of John's children,' I quavered, 'and I want you to know how I feel!' I handed you the letter and politely declined your offer of a cup of tea. I got to work and phoned John.

'Don't be so bitter, and pull yourself together,' he advised.

I tried to do just that. I tried desperately hard not to blame you for cementing the rift at the time when, for me, at least, reconciliation seemed a tangible reality.

Days went by, and I must admit, I didn't die. I carried on working, mothering, sleeping less and drinking a lot more than I used to. I even went to a party and felt quite normal for most of the evening. But then they played 'Red, Red Wine' at 1.30 in the morning and I crumbled and rang his—sorry, your—telephone number.

'Don't be so bitter,' he said, as I sobbed and pleaded into the receiver.

I could hear you humming contentedly in the background. I drove home in a stupor and cried until the sun rose.

The next time I saw you I had pulled myself together with the help of Valium and a nice man in a white coat. I wanted to know, adult to adult, how you visualised things would be with the children, seeing as they were used to spending weekends with their father. I discovered that you knew very little about anything—not even how many children there were, let alone their names. I tried to imagine them there, with you, with their father, and it all became too complicated to contemplate further.

I collected the mail as usual, once or twice a week, and couldn't help noticing that I was getting fewer and fewer letters whilst you—now calling yourself Mrs John Smith—were getting more and more. At the time it seemed highly significant. You were not only in our home, our garden, our bed and our kitchen but you were also in the little green rented postbox in town. I forced myself to carry on collecting the mail even though it hurt me more than anything else. When I realised that there were going to be no more letters for me in that box, I handed him back the key.

It's your key now. I know because I sometimes see your car outside the post office when I drive home from work. The first time I saw your car, I had this incredibly strong urge to swerve across the traffic and plough into it. This feeling increased to the point where I wanted to attack all VW Beetles regardless of the colour.

It was explained that this kind of feeling is quite normal and that it can be expected to diminish in a year or two. In the meantime, though, I wonder whether you and I should take out some kind of life insurance, just in case . . . ?

The next time I saw you, you were with him, getting into the car. I couldn't believe my luck. He had been avoiding me, and hadn't given me any maintenance money for the children for ages. I parked right behind your car and started hooting frantically when I noticed he was starting to pull away. I leapt out of the car and stuck my head through the open window.

'Got any money for me? We're flat broke and there are all these bills . . . ' I rattled.

You were hiding behind a huge bunch of white flowers, and John was tugging at his tie, looking flustered. He never wore a tie, and you didn't usually carry flowers, did you?

'No, no. I'll send you some money with the veggies in the truck this afternoon,' he mumbled. I caught a glimpse of your smile as you drove away. I used to smile too, then, in the first months of new love, before the harsh realities pushed their way into the foreground.

The next time I see you, I won't be bitter. I'll be just what I am—a single parent, a teacher, living in Zimbabwe. I'll be off the pills and I won't be seeing the nice man in the white coat any more. My hands will no longer shake when I drive past Beetles of all colours, and the sound of your name will just be like any other word.

Weep Not

(for Dambudzo Marechera)

by Barbara Makhalisa

Weep not
For the silent soulless shell
Cocooned in stone cold gloom

Worms are deaf-mute
To glorious eulogising
For them
This dark doom
Is bounteous boom

Blind is the boneyard
To this decorated mound
Clogged its nose
To the gaudy splendour
Yet not a petal
Graced my shabby shack
In sickness

Where was your care
When lonely I brooded
In my dreary dungeon
When my guts writhed
As hunger gnawed
At my heart strings

When thirst parched
My craving and cramping belly
Where was your fondness?

Your eyes shied away
From the shrunken shambles
And your present passion
Is but a fleeting cloud

But
My lines immortal sneer
At your sniffy snobbery

ZWW
Branches

Batsirai
Bulawayo & Mbizingwe
Chivu
Dendenyore
Goromonzi & Goromonzi North
Guruve
Gwanda
Harare
Hwange
Kushingirira
Mandedza
Mberengwa
Railway Block
Shurugwi Urban
Tinei
Tongogara
Zinatsa
**Is there a Branch
in your area?**

The Sack

by Norma Kitson

Alva Plein was so tired she just flopped onto the sofa and lit a Berkeley with her Dunhill lighter. The cigarette tasted dry and the smoke scratched the back of her throat. She put her hand to her forehead and it felt clammy. Alva sighed.

It had been a bad day: frustrating and irritating. A whole day at the Bridge Club and the Fun Pairs had not been fun at all. They'd come second bottom. Bridget was a really rotten player and Alva wondered why, with her aptitude for the game, she couldn't find a decent partner.

It's embarrassing really, someone like me, she thought, coming down so low. No matter how many times I tell that Bridget what conventions to play, she forgets. And now, just because I lost my temper with her over that last hand, she doesn't want to play with me any more.

Bill, looking tired and bashed out from his golf, appeared in the doorway: "Anything to eat? How was it? When did you get home? I'm hungry."

"You're always hungry," said Alva. "You *know* the Shonamatic's off on Sundays. So why don't you just go and get yourself a cheese sandwich or something—and get me a brandy and soda while you're about it."

"Bloody hell," said Bill. "That two-legged dishwasher's always off these days! He only just came back from his holiday! Well, can't you even make one bloody meal a week, for God's sake?"

"Look," said Alva, "I've had a helluva rotten day and I'm tired as hell. Why don't you just leave me alone."

Disconsolately she squashed out her cigarette in the glass ashtray. The roses in the lalique vase were wilting. The house was a mess. It was well into October and the fire was still laid. Ridiculous in this heat! By now there should be a great vase of flowers in front of the grate. It wasn't as if Joseph didn't know that. In the old days I'd have called up to his room and had him fix it immediately, but everything's changed—for the worse.

And now that the children were grown up and had left home, things between her and Bill were worse as well. Now, when there were no teenagers arguing and fighting, endlessly competing, squabbling and demanding, instead of growing closer, Bill and she had become strangers. He went to work, to golf, roamed around the house at night with insomnia, and suffered bouts of deep depression. He was always tired, boring really. Alva felt cheated.

She eased herself deeper into the sofa, unstrapped her new high-heeled sandals and swung her legs up onto the tapestry stool.

So many worries! Joseph would have to go. She couldn't remember a time without Joseph but he was no good any more. Before, he'd been quite happy and uncomplaining but now there was a constant moan from him about his children in rural Bindura. He was always asking for time off: someone was ill, or he had to go home to pick his mealies, fix the roof, and forever borrowing money for school fees. Always something!

Why, thought Alva, did they have so many children? It was so uncivilised. And now, if you don't mind, Joseph wanted time off to go to ZANU meetings!

Now they're running the country - and look what's happening. No sardines in the shops and you can never get rice when you want it. No olives, no olive oil. Every useful cent in the country's going on education at the cost of necessities. You give them freedom and equality and then they start rioting at the university. Thank God we had the sense to send our Barry to university in Cape Town, she thought. Whatever you want these days, you've got to go down South for it.

Bill appeared in the doorway again, propping his hand against the lintel. He handed her a drink.

"Are you going to sit there all night? Or are you going to go and get us something to eat?"

"Joseph will have to go," said Alva. "Tomorrow I'm going to give him the sack."

"Well, I don't mind," said Bill. "We have to cut down. Everything's going up in price and the expense of a domestic is killing. I've just got the account from Boy at the bottle store. It's over a hundred dollars. And the Greaterman's account for that new dress you wore to the Callinicos's anniversary - hell! And the water's gone up, never mind the phone. I wish you'd try to manage the house on your own now. After all, there's just the two of us."

"Trust you to think like that! You've been trying to chain me to the kitchen sink ever since we got married. I'm not going to spend the rest of my life as a drudge—whatever you think."

"Well, then," said Bill. "Put on your lipstick and we'll go over to the Haddons. They always have something to eat. She's a wonderful cook. You could take a lesson from Eileen, if you had any sense. Come on!"

"You go," said Alva. "I'm just going to have a bath, watch *Falcon Crest* and go to bed. I'm tired. I've had a helluva day. I can't eat anything else today. I'm putting on weight."

"Jesus!" said Bill, "You're getting so thin you're beginning to look scrawny. Where do you think this dieting is going to end?"

Alva turned her face away from him and Bill sat down on the riempie stool, elbows on knees and looked at her angrily.

56

"I've also had a rotten day, you know," he said. "Come *on*, Alva, let's go get something to eat."

"Perhaps we should have learned to speak Shona," Alva said. "There all the goings on: the students, the corruption, the drought, the electricity cuts, the President's speeches on the telly, and we can't understand a thing. I think they do it to annoy us."

"You know, she went on, "the price of houses is going up and up. Maybe we could sell up and go somewhere else. Australia, or England."

"And what do you think I'll be doing there? Bill asked. "I'd never get a job overseas. And anyway, how much do you think it'll cost to get a house in London or Sydney? And what about the weather? And you couldn't have a domestic there anyway."

Alva swung her legs up on the couch and lit another Berkeley.

"Its such rotten luck," she said. "There must be *somewhere* to go, *something* we can do."

She turned to face Bill, "I don't think I'll play Bridge at the Club anymore. I wish you'd learn to play, then we could have social Bridge at home. If only I could find a decent partner." She sat up. "Anyway, tomorrow I'm going to give Joseph the sack."

Bill ran his hand over his thinning hair: "Look! Do you think we could go and get something to eat now?"

She got up and walked past the gleaming oak and mukwa cabinets and tables, over the highly polished parquet floor with its vacuumed persian rungs, smoothed her beautifully ironed, pleated dress over her slim hips. She walked over to the french windows and looked out over the acre and a half of manicured lawn and beautifully laid out garden, across the glittering swimming pool at the neat flower beds and the jacaranda trees in full bloom.

Well out of sight, at the back of the house, behind the vegetable garden, outside the cold-water shack, Joseph sat alone, worried, cooking sadza over a few sticks.

Maybe, Alva thought, I should phone Bridget and

make friends again. Monday was League night at the Bridge Club, after all.

"Come on, then Bill," she called. "Let's go and pop in on the Haddons. They're bound to have something for you to eat."

She strapped up her sandals and resolutely stretched to her full height, running her fingers through her well-cut, glossy brown hair. "Come on, then, Bill."

It was just another shitty day in paradise.

For further information about Zimbabwe Women Writers publications and activities write to:

The Coordinator
Zimbabwe Women Writers
78 Kaguvi Street
Harare
Zimbabwe

Please cover postage costs

Seeds of Discontent

by Amanda Hammar

What's the matter with her?
She's a Jew who likes goys
a lesbian who likes men
and she mixes with blacks

Doesn't she know anything
about loyalty to her own?
(She's always been *dafke*)

How are we to trust her
with our fears
our secrets
(our bigotry)?

She's merging too much
Can't keep track of her
or define her
Can't see where the hell she IS

She's stepping over the line
you know
stepping out of line
getting dangerous
OUT OF CONTROL

We can't let her be seen
She'll poison our children's minds
Destroy our foundations
And sow seeds of discontent among us
Among us
AMONG US

The Secret Cave

by Ruth Gabi

Shingirirai walked alone from school very slowly. What the teacher had told them to do was impossible. She had no grandmother. How could she talk to her grandmother when she was dead? Who could she talk to? She had to write a page for her history project about an important woman in history. Grade Six work was difficult. She sighed.

She realised she had wandered far from the path. Something was wrong. It was too quiet. She must have gone the wrong way. She stopped. The Baobab tree in front of her seemed—yes—to be smiling! But that's silly. Trees don't smile! Somehow she was not afraid. The smiling mouth in the tree grew larger and larger:

'Well, there's no harm in going inside,' she thought to herself. It looked so inviting.

She stepped in and found herself in a huge cave. Gourds with clear, refreshing water hung from the roof. As she walked slowly forward, she heard singing from the back of the cave:

'Mbuya Nehanda! Mbuya Nehanda! Mbuya Nehanda! The water is boiling!'

There was a fire at the back of the cave. She went towards it. She could see six young women on their knees grinding maize. They were wearing brown cloths which reached their knees. The ends of each cloth were tied round the right shoulder. Their hair was plaited. One woman sat alone against the wall. She was dressed like the other women but was older and had very short hair. She spoke:

'Welcome, my child. Sit down and eat. While you are eating I will tell you about myself.'

Shingirirai looked at her again. She knew this woman. She had seen that face many times—those determined eyes. She felt her heart thumping. She trembled with excitement. She was face to face with Mbuya Nehanda!

Shingirirai hardly tasted the sadza and pumpkin leaves that were put before her. Her heart felt like bursting with joy. Here was her homework being done for her. Mbuya Nehanda was going to tell her about her life.

Oops! she choked. She must remember her manners and eat slowly. But this meeting was so exciting! Who would believe that she had met Mbuya Nehanda? Even she found it unbelievable.

'Yes, my child. I am Mbuya Nehanda, your grandmother, and the grandmother of your grandmother,' she said, smiling.

'But, but,' Shingirirai stammered, 'but you died. How can it be that you are here?'

'Ah! you are a bright child. Shh, and listen—this is the home of your ancestors and you will come out wise,' she whispered. 'Now I will begin my story,' she said slowly.

Somewhere far behind, in the cave, Shingirirai could hear mbira music.

'I have always been a fighter, like you,' said Mbuya Nehanda.

'I am only a little girl. I can't fight!'

'Ah! my child, now you *are* fighting. Struggling to learn is like waging a war. In the Chimurenga war, I stood up and told our soldiers: "The bullets of the white men will not harm you". Yes, that was to put courage in them. Your forefathers fought bravely against the white men.'

As she spoke, her eyes shone. There was a fire in them. Shingirirai hung on every word she spoke.

'Ambuya,' she asked, 'why were you fighting the white men?'

'Aha, you will do well in your learning. You ask questions. Land, my child, land! Our people everywhere, are one with the land. It is our life. The white men took our life.'

Shingarirai wondered if that was why her mother was always working with a hoe. To get life from the soil. That was it! Yes, she loved roasted green maize very much. It was so delicious!

Mbuya Nehanda continued: 'To get our land, we fought. "Only the land," I told the soldiers: "Do not touch the white men's property." They listened to the spirit of Chaminuka in me.'

Shingirirai gazed at her in wonder. This slim, mature woman with such wise eyes. She had so much wisdom and courage! Indeed, the fire in her eyes shone as she continued:

'But, my child, the white men had fire in their sticks. Ah! we fought, but they spat too much fire. The spirit bowed for a while—but only for a while. I died in the flesh, but my spirit lives on. Here *you* are the spirit of tomorrow. The white men only hanged my flesh, but I am alive in you.'

Oh, she was so wise! Shingirirai felt like hugging her.

'I knew my spirit would live on, so I sang and danced to my death,' Mbuya Nehanda said, smiling.

Suddenly the mbira music grew louder and the maize grinding women began chanting:

'Mbuya Nehanda! Mbuya Nehanda! The water is boiling, Mbuya Nehanda! The Chimurenga has started, Mbuya Nehanda! Chaminuka's bones are talking—'

The chanting grew louder and louder. Shingiriarai was surprised to find herself dancing and following in the footsteps of Mbuya Nehanda. She danced as if she knew the steps. She stamped her little feet just like Mbuya Nehanda was doing. The music began to fade.

'Now it is time for you to return,' said Mbuya

Nehanda stretching out for one of the gourds of water. She gave Shingirirai a drink. The water was sweet and refreshing. She hadn't even realised she was thirsty. She gulped the water at first and then drank more slowly. She must remember her manners. She really couldn't choke a second time!

'Farewell, my child. Remember, you are the new spirit!' Mbuya Nehanda said, patting Shingirirai on the shoulder.

One of the women who was grinding the maize stood up and led Shingirirai out. She walked as if in a dream. A mist surrounded her.

Suddenly she found herself alone, looking at the great Baobab tree—which winked—yes, winked at her. She frowned. It couldn't have. Oh this naughty tree! Shingirirai smiled. Her smile grew bigger. She looked right up at the tree and shouted gaily: 'Baobab tree, I know your secret!'

She did not wait for an answer. She was so happy. Her heart was full of joy. Her homework was complete. She wished she could tell her classmates what had happened. She wished tomorrow would come so that she could tell them the life of Mbuya Nehanda—well, not everything—but most of it. Who would believe her if she said that the great Baobab tree had smiled? That was her secret.

She clutched her bag and burst into song as she skipped home.

'Mbuya Nehanda! Mbuya Nehanda! Mbuya Nehanda! The water is boiling. Mbuya Nehanda! The Chimurenga has started!'

Curse

by Michelle Baker

Let no someone tell you
that this crimson tide
spills with it thrills
of fertility—

No.

Nothing but the drag
as brittle shells
and clinging seaweed
maul
the black and heavy sand

Why, why and all my womanly ambitions

by Gloria-Anne Francis

I would really like to know why I have to cook submissively, why I have to watch the pots passively, in case they might burn.

But I'm doing it anyway, so I gently take the ground mealies in the blue-dented, rusty tin that expresses pain and anguish through age on its outward look, and this is caused by the many years it has stood in our pantry.

I dig the green plastic saucer—that no longer has a matching cup—through the meal and thoughtfully turn to the sadza pot to fill it with more mealie-meal, as a finishing touch to the family dish.

But then, I suddenly realise something—something I have known for years but unfortunately have not realised until this day, until this very moment.

The realisation is the fact that the pot holding the sadza said nothing. I mean, nothing at all. The mgoti stick can only knock, knock, against the sadza to smooth it. And the sadza can only rumble, but in its own silence. All these utensils can not speak out what they feel. But the thing is, I can, but I never have. But after realising this, I have the incentive to defy society.

Right! Why should I cook just because it is supposed to be a phase of womanhood? Why can't little brother Trevor cook for himself and father. I learned, so can he.

I mean, why do I have to sit with my legs crossed, no matter what I am wearing? Why can I not sit the way I feel comfortable, even if my tremendous—or beastly large thighs can be seen.

Why can I not answer back, defy or question a man's doings. Why not? If he can me, then I certainly do not see why I can not him!

Why? Why should I resist confrontation with the opposite sex. Just because I am the opposite sex? Why? I am intelligent and rebellious enough to do so, but I have been timid for too long.

I want to tell a man exactly what I think, feel, wish, detest and like about him, without being reluctant or tense in doing so.

I want to explain to a man what an arrogant, selfish pig he can be at times. I do want to tell him—I really do—but, but, *but* in such a way he can appreciate the advice and accusations.

I want to be able to go to any bar in the city, alone, or with a group of females without being looked at with disfavour and being titled a prostitute.

Why can I not talk, laugh, joke and be around a man without making him have ideas of sounding me out with aesthetic romantic words, influencing a love affair for the future?

Last, but certainly not the least, I want to marry a man. I mean I do not want to be married by a man.

Why do men have to be the ones to sound out, propose or marry women. Why can't we women now be the ones to sound out, propose or marry men and live our married lives DEMOCRATICALLY—HAPPY!

Unspoken

by Amanda Hammar

we're drinking tea
and she asks
what are you

animal, vegetable, mineral
what's she asking

I mean are you married single divorced
or what

same kind of question
I suppose
but it's none of the above
why don't I say
it's on the tip of my tongue

I sip from my cup
she offers me
another slice of cake

Leopard Rock

by Michelle Baker

(While visiting the Vumba, Michelle (from New Zealand) was told
that women, in tribal times, were taken to the top of Leopard Rock and
thrown off as punishment for crimes).

i am the rock
the spirit of the killers
the ghost of the dead
i am the one
I alone have the memory
so colourful
too loud to turn their falling
into flight
heaving for their breath
they laboured
some fell on their knees
the ground so steep
inside their strong
and shaking limbs
the blood burned bright
against the wind
and soon a life they thought
so soon to splash
this greyblack hill
the bluewhite sky
for guilt or innocence
echoes tumbling
in the vast receding valley
i am the leopard
i crouch
i wait

Uphill

by Cornelia Bullen-Smith

As she reached for the cup of hot, strong coffee, she felt a wave of desperation building up. Sisyphos stood next to her near the wall with the broken glass. She watched him knowingly and with sisterly compassion as, grunting, he picked up the enormous marble rock that had rolled down, and began pushing it back up the hill.

'This is not the day to get bogged down again,' she decided, taking another sip of coffee.

'Beautiful sunshine, blue sky, birds singing in the trees full of flower-colours. I'll manage, damn it all.' She got up and went into the house.

She dialled the dentist and postponed her appointment to a day when she'd have money to pay for it. She rang the doctor and arranged to see him for a check-up. Done, and ten minutes of her three free morning hours gone. Next, the beds.

As she threw herself into organising the rooms: picking up toys and dirty clothes, putting things back in their places—doing all the tidying and cleaning she thought had to be done to make the home welcoming for the other three members of her family—a puzzling sharp image from Friday afternoon assailed her:

It was prize-giving day at their daughter's school. As they waited for the celebration to begin, she watched the headmistress walk past, her breasts bouncing under the floral design of her dress like tennis balls out of control. She saw the fat man follow the bouncing balls all the way past the parents and invited guests . . .

The telephone rang. She took down a message for her husband. The kitchen clock confirmed that ninety minutes of her morning had evaporated. As she let hot water run into the sink to wash the dishes, she looked out of the window and caught a glimpse of Sisyphos halfway up the hill, sweating profusely. She turned away and switched on the radio.

Cleaning the dishes, one by one, becoming aware of her sore legs and aching back, she remembered gratefully that she'd done the laundry and shopping yesterday—some free minutes collected and saved up for today. If she hurried, fed the dogs and quickly cleaned out the guinea pig cage, she might be able to add another few minutes to those saved from yesterday.

'What would you *really* like to do with your life?' the voice on the radio asked.

'Oh,' she thought, as she opened a can of dogfood, 'what a question! Play tennis, swim, run for fun, sleep, write, watch people, listen, teach, read, listen to music...'

She filled the dogbowls and straightened up slowly. 'No,' she thought, as the radio played music again, 'for starters it would be nice just to sit and discover who I am. I have lost myself in all these years of housework and bringing up the children. Before the birth of the first child, I could look into the mirror and see *me*. Now I can't see that Me any more. I must have changed over the years. I never have any time to look for myself.'

She picked up the guinea pig cage, carried it outside and set it down carefully. Looking around for the scrubbing brush, she heard a groan of despair.

Sisyphos had almost reached the top of the hill. He staggered. Knowing what would happen next, she started running towards him. Panting, out of breath, she ran and struggled and ran.

'It's me,' she shouted as Sisyphos turned to her. 'I'll help you—it's me! This time the rock will not roll back. This time, I'll be there.

She got there just in time.

70

Fight On!

by Barbara Makalisa

'It's not fair
Not fair at all.'
My girlie
Who promised it would be?

It is the same
Exactly the same
You've got to fight it.
My grandma fought it
With quiet resilience she won the battle.

Her dad had said,
'School is for lads.
You can now write your name
You can read the Bible too.
Soon, you will marry
And you won't mind me in old age.'

Grandma fled from home.

The next they heard
She worked at a mission station
To earn her keep and schooling.
Her dad died in her gentle hands.

In marriage
It was the same,
Exactly the same.

The first man kicked her out
For being barren.
Her second and third wives were barren too.
Grandpa married Grandma
They had Dad
And Dad had me.

Mama fought it too
For it was the same,
Exactly the same, if not worse.
Nine months and duck waddling
Yet she cleaned, laundered,
Cooked and served daily.
She cared for us in sickness and distress
She sowed, cultivated and harvested
Her wages were insults all around.

When I excelled, Dad sang a song.
When I failed, Mama was to blame.

Dad died and Mama was the witch
The greedy sharks stripped her clean.
They swallowed flesh, bone and marrow.
But, armed with education
She started from scratch and blossomed.

I have fought it too, my girlie
For it has been the same,
Exactly the same, if not worse still.

Though I am equally qualified
I cannot be on par.
'Their main task should be baby production
Should machines take leave while they tend babies?'

Once I almost registered promotion
But it went to more permanent staff.
'As long as you go on maternity leave
You can never hope to march up the career ladder
Your lot will be low wages and low status!'

When I wished to exercise birth control
For the good of my health and my children's
'She wants to prostitute
Send her away!'

When my emancipated sister
asserts her capabilities
She earns scorn and is also branded a prostitute.
'She's not a woman this one
Look at the way she addresses men!
She'd rather sit and be served tea.
She drives round the country alone
Books into hotels alone
While her man tends the children!
Ugh!
If she were mine
I would straighten her with a stick.'

It is the same my girlie
Exactly the same.

My friend could not be employed for months
Not for lack of suitable qualifications.
She refused to heed the Wolf's smile
Refused to be patted and dated
Refused to wine and dine with the boss
Refused to compromise her integrity.
Mind,
Her refusal earned her lasting respect.

Another colleague suffered the same
Exactly the same.

She was lured and raped in broad daylight.
When she reported the crime
The court tried her instead.
'You invited it, madam, didn't you?
Is it because he paid you too little?
You have a grudge against him, eh?
Don't dither, tell us exactly what he did.'

It is still the same
Exactly the same, my girlie.

Take up arms and wage war
Let your spear be education
Let your shield be knowledge
Let 'Truth at all times' be your motto
Let your will be the determination to work hard
For sisters illiterate still abound
Fight it to enlighten them
Fight it by solidarity of purpose
The nation cannot develop
Without your participation.

Grandma fought it
Mama fought it
I still fight it
You have to fight it
Your daughter will have to fight it

Fight on!

Please say yes

by Memory Dete

Chidhakwa was seated at the back of the beerhall. In his hands he held a big, brown mug of 'chibuku'. Absent-mindedly he shook the mug vigorously before taking it up to his eager lips. Lost in his thoughts concerning 'amai' Nhamo whom he loved dearly, Chidhakwa was oblivious of the loud noise in the beerhall.

Amai Nhamo was a tough nut to crack and he knew that it was not going to be easy to convince her to marry him. She had loved her husband dearly and had told him that she would remain a widow for the rest of her life.

'There is no other man for me in this world except Tichafa,' she said firmly when he first approached on this issue.

Chidhakwa hoped that this time he would succeed in convincing her that it was an unwise choice to remain a widow. He had to make her realise that she was still too young to consider shelving the idea of re-marrying.

As he trudged through the bushes and long, dry grass, he pictured amai Nhamo's face and smiled silently to himself. He soon arrived at the rundown homestead and before entering the hut where she and her son were having their afternoon meal, he took off his dusty boots and hat then walked in.

He was given a warm welcome but declined the offer to join in the meal. Though he explained that he was hungry, the real truth was that he did not wish to waste time by having something to eat as he wanted to get straight down to the nitty gritty.

He waited shortly as Nhamo and his mother finished their meal before he brought out the clothes he had bought for them. 'These are for you and your son,' he said, handing the bundle to her. He watched her closely as she took them from him and held them up one by one: the skirts, dresses, shorts and pairs of trousers. She was very close to tears of happiness when she looked at him and all her thankfulness was written on her face.

'I don't know how to thank you,' she said. 'Nhamo and I badly needed clothes but I wish you had not troubled yourself.'

She took a black clay pot from the fireplace and removed its lid. She peered inside. 'There are a few pumpkins left over from this morning,' she told him. 'Shall I give you some? It would not be right if you walked away without having eaten anything.'

Chidhakwa shook his head. 'Don't worry about me,' he assured her. 'I have had my favourite food already.'

'How could I forget?, amai Nhamo laughed, and became serious again. 'Beware that you do not develop an illness from your heavy drinking.'

I am not a heavy drinker,' Chidhakwa defended himself.

'If you aren't a heavy drinker, then how come you earned yourself the nickname "Chidhakwa"?'

Chidhakwa did not like the sudden turn of conversation. He had not visited amai Nhamo so that she could remind him about his drinking habits. He had to switch the conversation back to its original course but he could not do so with young Nhamo in the room. He took a few coins from his pocket and gave them to the boy whose face lit up immediately. At his mother's orders Nhamo collected the plates which they had eaten from and

76

put them outside to be washed later, then bounded off to the shops to spend his money. Chidhakwa waited until Nhamo was well out of earshot before speaking:

'Amaiguru,' he began. 'How long is it now since Tichafa's death?'

Amai Nhamo had not been prepared for the sudden question. She took long to respond and fought back tears, then bravely responded. 'It is now two years.'

'Is two years not long enough to have re-married?' he asked her. 'You hardly have enough food to eat, little clothing, and you know that I can provide these necessities for you, but you are stubborn enough to keep turning me down.'

Amai Nhamo's mind went back to the day that she and Tichafa had announced their intention to marry. Chidhakwa had been wild because he had hoped to marry her himself. Now that Tichafa was dead, he dared to think that she would embrace his desires. How wrong his thoughts were!

Chidhakwa was considered to be rich by village standards and if she agreed to marry him she would bid farewell to poverty for good. To many she was a fool to let this chance slip by but she knew that Chidhakwa was not for her. He would never be faithful, because next in line to beer, his favourite pastime was pursuing women. He had never married but had indulged in many indiscretions, resulting in his having seven children—all from different mothers.

Another reason why amai Nhamo could never agree to marry Chidhakwa was because he was her chief suspect in the cause of her husband's mysterious death from poisoning. She held no proof and had not told anyone of her suspicion, but strongly believed that he was somehow implicated in Tichafa's sudden death.

From the stool where he sat, Chidhakwa saw the tears brimming in amai Nhamo's eyes. He knew that he had stirred sad memories which time had healed, and he debated on whether to continue with his proposal or forget about it completely.

For several seconds the room hung in silence before Chidhakwa spoke again. He had come to convince amai Nhamo to marry him and this he decided he must do.

'You know that I was in love with you before Tichafa met you,' he said gently. 'You allowed yourself to be whisked away from me but the time has come when you should return back to me.'

He looked towards her for a positive response and she stared down at the gift of clothes which he had presented to her. She knew now that he had aimed at buying her love. That was indeed a shame because she had believed the kind gesture was out of the goodness of his heart. When she spoke, her voice was firm.

'I refuse to marry you, Babamudiki. I do not know what the future holds in store for me because as you keep reminding me, I am not an old woman and can marry again. But it can never be you.'

Disbelief, then anger, showed itself clearly on his face and he unconsciously clenched his fists. When he stood up, a wave of fear gripped amai Nhamo. She feared that he would strike her, but was relieved when he walked to the door and said to her: 'Goodbye for now. But I will not give up easily.'

Then he walked unsteadily out of the room.

When he arrived home he threw himself across the bed and allowed the alcohol and his disappointment to lull him to sleep. He was awakened later by a gentle knock on his door. 'Who is it?' he asked sleepily, not sure whether he was awake or dreaming.

'It is me, Baba,' his eldest daughter replied. Chidhakwa looked at his watch and was amazed to see that it was almost ten o'clock. He had slept for over five hours!

He took the tray of food and dismissed his daughter. He ate his supper absentmindedly, without really being aware of what was on his plate. In his mind he re-lived the moment when he had become aware that he had lost amai Nhamo to Tichafa. His brother had walked up to him with a big grin and shattered his dreams: 'Go and buy your best suit Tongai (as Chidhakwa had been known then) because I want you to be my best man. Shingai has agreed to marry me.'

Chidhakwa had glared at Tichafa for several seconds before giving him a blow which sent him sprawling to the ground. With surprise and fury matching his, Tichafa had leapt up and soon the two brothers were engaged in a fierce fight. Fortunately a neighbour arrived at the scene and put a stop to the fight. What he managed to stop was the fight, but not the hatred which had sprung up between the two brothers.

Chidhakwa had begun leading a careless life which resulted in heavy drinking and smoking and he earned the nickname "Chidhakwa". His hatred for Tichafa grew until it was a sore in his heart. Each day it grew to greater proportions and at length he decided to leave the village and migrated to the city.

He returned to the village a few years later and with the wealth he had accumulated from working in the city, he built two supermarkets at the village growth point. On the other hand Tichafa was struggling to make ends meet and Chidhakwa hoped that this would tempt Shingai to leave him. As the years passed and this did not happen Chidhakwa began to think of other ways of winning Shingai.

His love for Shingai had been so intense that he was driven to commit murder and, in doing so, he had lost everything. He had lost his brother and still failed to win Shingai. It was now obvious to him that he would never win her. The only thing left to do was to confess.

It was a most difficult thing to do but it had to be done. The guilt of his responsibility for Tichafa's death was becoming heavier and heavier. Amai Nhamo had to learn the truth. Her refusal to marry him had enlightened him on how devilishly he had behaved and that his confession was now the only relief he would find from his burdens. When the next day dawned he would make known the skeleton in his cupboard.

Chidhakwa did not wait for breakfast the following morning. As soon as he awoke, he made his way to amai Nhamo's house.

Nhamo was milking the cows and he stopped to greet the young boy as he passed by. Nhamo told him that his mother had gone to the well and Chidhakwa went inside the hut and waited for her to return. Moments later she came back with a can of water balanced on her head. She was unaware of him but he watched her intently. When she turned to find him looking straight at her she was annoyed but managed to greet him politely. He explained to her that he had something to say and she spread the reed mat on the floor and sat down to listen.

'It is no secret that Tichafa and I were enemies right to his death,' he began. 'Through all his living years, I tried to win you from him but this failed and when he died, I thought that you would not hesitate to marry me. But this again proved fruitless. I am now realising painfully that Tichafa's death did not gain me the happiness I was bargaining for.'

Amai Nhamo was relieved that he seemed to be accepting defeat at last but she felt hurt that he had actually been happy over Tichafa's death. The hatred between them had been so intense!. She looked up to find Chidhakwa watching her and looked down again in embarrassment. Chidhadkwa went on:

'I want you to know that I regret the enmity between me and my brother. If I could change the hands of time I would re-wind them to the days Tichafa was alive and we would try to patch up our differences. I have this great weight upon me because of his death and I don't think anyone can lift it from my shoulders.'

It was apparent that Chidhakwa had a great confession to make, yet he seemed hesitant to make it. There was also doubt that the confession had something to

80

do with her husband's death. Had her suspicions then been well-founded? Had Chidhakwa really been involved in bringing about Tichafa's death?

Chidhakwa avoided her questioning gaze and toyed with his hat. He hesitated before bursting out the truth. Even though amai Nhamo had suspected him, it did not stop her from being stunned.

A deathly silence followed before she filled the room with racking cries which were mingled with curses directed to Chidhakwa.

Nhamo heard his mother's cry and ran into the hut to see what was happening. Neighbours who heard the screams, thinking that a death had occurred, hurried to the scene and a hysterical amai Nhamo unfolded the story.

Chidhakwa knew that there was no escape. Surprisingly he remained calm and was not in the least bit afraid. For the past two years he had lived a life of fear because of the frightening nightmares he suffered at night. The most frightening of them was the one in which Tichafa chased him through a dense forest holding a glittering razor sharp knife. In this nightmare Chidhakwa always managed to evade Tichafa but when he thought he was safe, a river suddenly appeared out of nowhere and a strong gust of wind threw him right into the middle of it. Spluttering and trying to keep afloat he came face to face with a giant menacing crocodile. It opened its jaws and his loud anguished screams jolted him out of sleep to find himself wet with perspiration.

When one of the elderly neighbours—who decided to take charge of the situation—asked him whether amai Nhamo's accusations were correct, he nodded dumbly.

That same morning, after Chidhakwa was whisked off to the police station, amai Nhamo packed all her clothes. She did not doubt that her parents would welcome her and Nhamo to their village. She did not care what became of Chidhakwa. He would deserve whatever sentence they gave him. In her parent's village, she would make a new start.

Realisation

✟

by Press Sibanda

Seeing him lying in the naive dignity of death
I stood, arrested in fear and respect.
I felt countermanded.
How inviolable he lay in himself.
I had nothing to do with him now.
I could not accept it.

I embraced his dead body with my lips:
I put my hands on his face and murmured incoherently
My tears fell in succession
As drops from wet leaves.
I listened inquiringly, trying to get some connection,
But he was impregnable.

His mouth had fallen back, slightly open.
My womb went cold with fear.
He was a stranger
With whom I had been living as one flesh.
Was this all it meant—
Utter, intact separateness? In dread,
I turned away in unbearable pain.

I was rigid with agony.
I had the children to look after
I knew I was committed to life
For life was my immediate master.
But from death, my ultimate master,
I winced with fear and respect.

Mbuya

by Christine Rundofa

My grandmother is the most interesting person I know—old, withered, but wise. Her skin is a dark chocolate-brown and, because of all the creases on it, it looks like a raisin. Her eyes are like sunken holes set just above her strong jutting cheekbones. Those eyes look as if they have seen more than they should and if you look straight into them, it's like sinking into a deep well and not knowing what you will find. Her hair, with its wisps of white, is short and uncombed, on top of a head which seems too big for her frail neck and body.

She is about 90, and was born in Chivhu. When she comes to visit us in town, she always makes sure that we do not wear trousers, shorts or minis. At breakfast, she sits on the floor and fills her cup with sugar. She loves to sit in front of the fire or heater in winter and summer, no matter how hot our summers might be. During this time by the fire or heater, she takes lumps of sugar that she has made herself—by placing sugar in a tray and dampening it with a little water. Then she places the tray in the sun for the water to evaporate. When that is done, she breaks the sugar up into lumps which she always sucks. My grandmother does not have teeth any more, so we either buy or make mincemeat for her—but she prefers to have no meat at all.

When my grandmother sits in the sun and takes out her snuffbox—which is just an old tin of camphor rub—we know that this is a sign to show that she is contented. Then we join her and sit and listen to her as she compares our modern days to her old ones.

Every evening we have to say a bible verse, one we know by heart, or one we love, and that will be our thought for the day. She does not like lazy people and enjoys watering the garden with tin cans—not a hose-pipe! She prefers to sit on the floor whenever men are in the room, as this is the traditional custom.

One thing she hates is being cold—and another is seeing people hurt. She loves sitting by herself in a quiet corner and when she is at home we complain that she makes us work too much. But when she is gone, we miss her. When she comes, she brings us traditional or African fruits, or meat, which we love.

When she leaves, we all say a prayer, and she is the one who chooses and conducts it. We all say a thanks. She is so scared of the television set—heads with no bodies talking—so we watch the one in the bedroom.

Sometimes she complains about being lonely and missing the noisy games played by the kids back home, so the whole family, including my parents, come and join in the games she teaches us, just to show her we love her—but she is annoying at times.

My grandmother is definitely the most interesting person I know.

The Me The World Doesn't See

by Shingirai Pensado

I am like every woman you see—
Fit, and strong in mind
Always scratching my head
Like a fork scraping a pot of porridge
To find new ideas
And memories of the past.

The world always shuns me
When I try to raise a point.
(It's like I'm cutting meat with a blunt knife)
Everyone turns a deaf ear.

My heart always pumps.
There is no day. Life is dull
I see black night everywhere.
Life to me is constant.

I am beautiful as a nut,
But who can see my beauty
When I am covered by a shell?
Who will break the shell for me?

I am longing to see the sun.
I've been mature for ages.
I'm smooth as an olive—
As bright as a glowing candle.

Sizzling Notoriety

by Judy Monkhouse

Mrs van Rensberg's legs stuck out from under the car like a V-shaped plump, pale pork sausage. They twisted and turned in conjunction with her grunts and turned a nasty pink in the hot sun as she ground her feet, clad in tattered tackies, into the soft earth.

Her yard was strewn with the odd carcass or two of cars with dents, smudges of naartjie coloured rust and broken windscreens with large, gaping, open-mouthed holes. Exposed to the elements, children and dogs, were chairs with dirty yellow foam stuffing, torn sections revealing coils of metal springs sagging after their abandonment.

Although aware of their sizzling notoriety, Mrs van Rensberg didn't give a damn. We had to pass her house, mornings and afternoons, on the way to and from school and peered through the gaps in the hedge, which was covered in powdery dust, for a glimpse of her.

'Do as you're told Kaffirrr!' she screeched.

She appeared from the recesses of the house in the same faded printed cotton with dirt marks around her hips where her hands were permanently fastened as she gave out orders to indolent servants.

She spat. I saw her myself—a long stream of spittle reached an impressive distance of several yards, accompanied by a 'Thisst!' Her hair was a mess of untidy curls and her blue eyes narrowed to angry or intense calculating slits.

She was clever. Who else could explain how a white woman could drag herself under an old Morris Oxford, get grease on her hands, her face, her dress and expose those porky legs, or even offer a peek at soft, white, marshmallow thighs to passers-by?

Many rumours circulated about her and the worst was that she wore no broeks. Thus, on the hot and laborious walk home from school we chose to stop for longer than we should outside Mrs van Rensberg's tangled yard, hoping to catch a glimpse of her working under the car—and with no broeks on. We were never sure. Our eyes strained and squinted through the resilient hedge to see if her legs were really parted and if there was a dark patch that could be ascribed to be her Adam and Eve.

'She's wriggling out!' someone would say, and that was enough to get us scampering away before the formidable woman could smash us with an insult.

Most of her children were as pink as their mother and if Mr Van ever existed we never saw him. We did a head count of seven bare-footed Afrikaners. The menagerie included scruffy chickens, bellicose dogs and a goat tethered in the back yard that had in all probability caused those perforations in the sheets on the line.

There was only one person out of place in that household: a thin, teenage girl often sat on the verandah reading. She was pale-pale, and wore her blonde hair long: tresses of silk like a frail, lonely picture-book princess. When we passed, she put her book down and stared at us but not in an unfriendly way—reaching across the colour lines with her light blue eyes in an unspoken acknowledgement.

We speculated wildly about her. She would fall in love with a coloured boy and her mother would threaten to run her down with the Morris Oxford. Or her mother would lock her in a room, pushing plates of boerewors through the door until she came to her senses. Or she

87

would run away with her lover. But where to? Finally, we settled on Beira because we heard that there was no colour-bar there. In the house along the beach they would raise dusky children with blonde streaks through their hair and learn to speak Portuguese and eat octopus and squid cooked with chillies.

Her lover, we decided, could not be too dark, so we settled on my friend Maureen's brother who was olive in complexion and drove the girls wild because he had green eyes. His hair was tightly frizzy although we decided that it being brown was an advantage. That settled the matter. Their children's hair would be acceptably wavy.

'You kids bugger off!' Mrs Van interrupted our miscegenation game, the prefix implying a flaw, some fatal error of mankind, a staining of one's honour like— mistake, misappropriation, misgiving, misanthropic or misogyny, or misfit.

Stubborn Fact

by Shilla Ndlovu

Like a needle, it pierces.
Like a spear, it stabs.
Like a prickly-pear, it prickles
It touches the roofs and borders
Of my mind
And proceeds deeper still.
No matter how hard I push it off.
It remains stubborn
Stubborn and painful
—That's what a Fact is!

<u>Insecurity</u>

by Press Sibanda

The feeling of danger and insecurity
That surrounds you
Gradually creeps into your heart
Sharpening your eyesight and hearing.
Your body, sensing danger,
Activates a certain secret signalling system.
Your mind feverishly searches
For an explanation
For this inner discomfort
And you begin to notice the gloomy
Unsmiling faces,
Deliberate
Nervous gait
And the distrustful look
In the eyes of passers-by.
You involuntarily watch yourself, thinking
Something strange,
Obscure
And new to you
Is going on here.

Madhlodlo Beergarden

by Chiedza Msengezi

On Saturdays when the sky is high and blue, the sun a sharp direct blaze, Madhlodlo Beergarden is a packed beehive. Stemming from within is a steady hum of tongues loosened with alcohol.

As Tembi walks closer to the gate, the hum heightens. There is a good feeling in the air. More people are arriving. Men—in polished shoes, pressed shirts and enough money in their inner jacket pockets to eat and drink. They arrive on foot from the surrounding hostels, from beyond Makokoba, in Emergency Taxis with splintered windscreens and tyres worn down to threads. Twenty years back one of them could have been her father, for he always ended up at Madhlodlo whenever he went out to 'stretch his legs,' 'buy a newspaper' or 'get some cigarettes'—some of his many euphemisms for going out to drink.

Now standing at the edge of the gate of the beergarden, Tembi is pleased with herself. She has a chance to satisfy her suspicions. An ill-omened place for a woman is what she has grown to believe the beergarden to be. Once, she asked her husband to accompany her.

'What would somebody's *wife* be looking for in such a place!?' Her husband was puzzled by her interest. He offered an alternative. 'Wait until I get enough money to take you to a decent hotel.'

She wanted to say, 'I am fed up with quiet,' but did not want to start an argument. Today her husband has not been obstructive. It is a club project to explore Makokoba.

A butcher is strategically located at the mouth of the beergarden. Barbeque fires are burning, yellow tongues fuelled by fatty drippings from the roasting meat are leaping into the air. Men are queuing up for a turn at the fires.

Hesitantly, Tembi steps inside, her eyes sweeping across the garden. What a world! The concrete floor is not thick with spilt beer, broken glass and cigarette ends. Scrubbed clean. No shattered windows. No scribbled walls. No toppled benches. Impeccable. Airy. In the Saturday broiling heat, this is the place to be. Tembi walks about, casting glances every which way. Men are sitting territorially in circles, talking and nodding at each other.

'Good brew!' says the one, hugging a mug-pint of frothing traditional beer.

'Umm. . . Umm. . .' The others grunt in agreement. Their mouths are full of barbequed offal, cucumber, tomatoes, onions and chillies. Healthy drinkers on a balanced diet. Tembi finds it hard to connect these fathers with the children out there with orange coloured hair and bloated tummies from lack of such food.

She looks for somewhere to sit. Gender seems to be important here. Detached from the drinkers is a group of women. There are elderly women, sitting on the floor arranging cucumbers, carrots and vegetables for sale. Two more women arrive with pots of steaming sadza, chicken pieces, yellow with Madras curry. They spread mealie-meal bags on the floor and join the others. With nothing to sell, Tembi does not join them.

She examines the crowd closely. Two women are snugly planted among the men. Tembi is assessing whether to join them when she notices the men are looking in her direction. Her uneasiness must have communicated itself. They are eyeing her up and down mistrustfully. Their looks seem to say, 'You do not promise pleasure.'

Without brightly coloured beads around her neck or large hoops dangling from her ears, she is unwelcome. There is a murmur. Another. Yet another. Like a roused swarm, they alert each other that here is an intruder. They buzz furiously with tongues, white hot with venom.

'*Heyi zviri kufambaseiko apo!*'

'*Palo mfazilo!*'

'*Pane mukadzi wekwamushe—mushe!*'

One stands up: 'If you don't want this,' he shouts above the rest, rubbing his fingers with his thumb to symbolise money, '*get out! VOETSEK!*'

Tembi feels defenceless against the ridicule and obscenities. Panicky, she runs away from her own weakness, tripping over her voluminous skirts, inwardly screaming at herself for not being able to face a world she has always wanted to know.

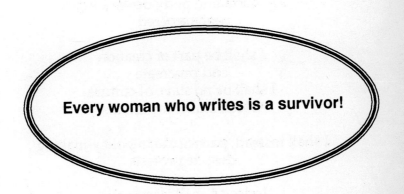

Every woman who writes is a survivor!

Product of Nature

by Lilian Masitera

I shall strip my face bare
of make-up
I shall watch my wrinkles and flaws
appear

I shall peel my stilettos and stockings
off my feet
My waist shall loosen
from fashionable girdles

Watch me walk gracefully
and eat my fill
My mind and body developing
unhampered

I shall be part of creation
and procreate
I shall be no slave of culture
which stunts my talents

I shall instead, participate in policy-making
despite protests

Indeed I shall stand solid
legs parted
to give life

But never to pleasure a partner
who thwarts my growth

Living Speech

by Peldah Hove

Speech vapours like morning dew
And vanishes like water in steam.
Speech loses shape with voice,
Exaggerated or under-reported, then passed.
Speech lives a life of eternity
Only when preserved in royal print.
Many traditional histories were buried
And passed—the arts unrecorded.
Masterpieces of oral tales and language
Geniuses of spoken poetry and verse
Factors of true historical resources
Legends of traditional heroes.
Eras of female subordination lapsed
Their great achievements sunk, unfelt.
Expertism in women's literature, vapoured
Orally showered as invisible tears—
Tears with no drop for the eye to note
While men wrote on men and were noted
While man wrote against woman and none challenged
Today the aspired sun has dawned for women
Come alive, women, in the immortal words of print
That tale, that poetry, social grievance—all of it!
Get it down and literature will judge your worth
Lay down your voice in print for an eternal echo

Don't fear error. Write it down.
For she who never blundered never ventured
And she who never ventured never gained
Pick up that pen and tell it all to us
Tell it all,
Tell it!

Unseen, therefore Nameless

by Megan Allardice

At the end of a day
Of uncertainty and pain
We come here
To find one another
Lose ourselves in warmth
Of blankets and bodies,
And thinking of sleep
I find you
Suddenly alive beside me
Find myself
Arching with need.

The record,
Caught in its groove
Chants a soft mantra,
And we two
Are not in a rut
But rutting.
Eventually our rocking
Must unbudge the record,
Release it to its own crescendo

Afterwards,
After whatever fluttering
Or aching climax we achieve,
We do not look,
Cinemalike,
Into each other's eyes,
Do not smile with light
Or lightness,
Do not risk to see there
The joy
Or tenderness
Or simply nothing.

Let the eye not trespass
Where the body
Has already staked its claim.

CAPTURE OUR ORAL TRADITION

Zimbabwe Women Writers see as their task
the recording of the oral story-telling tradition
of our people.

1. We encourage story-telling
2. We record stories on cassette
3. We write up the tales

Our elders hold the history of the country
and its peoples in stories passed down from
generation to generation.

We need tape recorders and basic writing
materials to enable our writers to go into the
rural areas to do this vital work.

The Decision

by Patience F. Dobha

The kind nurse gently wipes my brow and smiles at me. I have been a very good patient, she says—unlike the others she has had to put up with all week. I try to smile back but it doesn't quite reach my eyes.

She tells me that I have a baby girl and asks do I feel strong enough to hold her? Because for a moment I had allowed myself to forget, I'm shocked back into reality by her question. After a slight hesitation I nod my head.

As I wait for her to return, I feel panic start to well up inside of me and I press my eyes tightly shut to stop the threatening tears from spilling over. I feel a burning ache as I try to swallow the dry lump in my throat. A million questions go buzz in my head. What if she looks like him? What if she is abnormal and has the same beady little eyes? Would I have the courage to hold her—to keep her? What if I let that childless couple in Chitungwiza have her? Perhaps I should just twist the little neck till there is no life and then, like many girls before me, wrap it in a plastic bag.

Woman! Am I a woman now? But no, I'm only sixteen and so I'm still a child. But then again, who cares about my age? The fact that I now have a baby—as far as the world is concerned—means I have indulged in 'adult play' and am therefore a woman. But he demanded that I use no contraceptive. He said he didn't do it to me because he wanted to but that the spirits demanded it: that they had to be appeased. For a long time I had believed him so much that sometimes I'd even looked forward to the nights. Now, I wanted to cut him into little pieces.

It was after the dinner plates had been dried and put away and all twelve of my thirteen member family were seated in the lounge that the pains had started. The room was tiny with all of us in it. Present was my mother, third wife to my father. She treated all eleven of us children well. But during the past seven months after I started 'to show', she had avoided all eye contact with me and spoke in monosyllables. Was she afraid that the hate and disgust she felt towards me would show and be mirrored in her eyes? I looked at her expressionless face as she went on with her knitting. She was making some yellow thing that looked like a shawl. But I don't know much about those things because I'm only sixteen.

    As I continued to look at her, the hate I harboured towards her seemed to fade away. I was hateful towards her because she hadn't protected me the way a mother should. She had let him touch me. She had let him do this to me. To touch my secret places. To pant and heave and sweat and lunge at my body. She had let me almost enjoy being with him. And yet she had pretended not to see, not to know and in the tiny two bedroomed house, with its paper-thin walls, not to hear.

    But when I looked at her a little closer, I saw a helpless manipulated woman who had had her position of wife and mother turned into a farce. She had no education and for her, being a married woman had once been the ultimate ambition. I wanted to go to her and wrap her in my arms the way she used to do when I needed solace. I wanted to say gentle things to her to take a little of her hurt away.

    I thought I would end it all. So many times I had stood over his prostrate form with an axe in my hand and once I had even raised it above my head.

At the hospital they said I was 'small' and had to have a caesar. I was glad because I liked to think of 'it' as having been ripped from within me.

The nurse comes back with the bundle in her arms and again I try to smile at her, but my eyes feel dead. She places it on my chest with: 'Here's your mum now' and again tears threaten to roll. They irritate me because I had thought myself dried up. I ask the kind nurse please to leave us alone.

For a long moment I sit without looking down at the bundle that seems to be curiously looking around at this strange new world that isn't as warm as her previous home. But I am in no hurry to liberate her from the yellow wrap that covers her. I don't have the courage.

As she gives an impatient whimper, she fascinates me and with trembling hands, I slowly begin to unwrap her. First I see one tiny foot and then the other. The small body becomes very still as I go about my inspection. As I remove the shawl from her head, the most beautiful pair of black eyes on a snow white background look up at me. They view me unblinkingly, challenging me not to fall in love with her. Then a different kind of fear settles in. What if she decides I am not what she expected?

We look at each other critically and in silence. Slowly I pick her up and hold her close to me. I tell her she is the most beautiful baby in the world. I press her gently against me and set the tears free.

It wasn't her fault. But how much was it mine, since I had just given birth to my own sister?

More Than One Drought

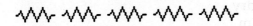

by Megan Allardice

Know that beneath
The prosperously sealed surface
Of First Street Mall
The ground is cracking,
As everywhere,
In webbed patterns.

In my house
Two men argue over possession
Of a pint of beer.
They thirst
Like the earth
For a few sacred drops
Of moisture
I notice
When the dispute is settled
That none is spared
For the ancestors.

We queued this year
For mealiemeal and love,
Salt and respect.
Mealiemeal and salt
Are now back on the shelves:
The drought still causes
Shortages
In the emotional supermarket.

People of the land
Turn away from the land
Turn to the borehole
Of a neighbour's compassion
And find it dry,
Turn to a dam
Of state providence
And find it stagnating,
Walk on in search
Of other sources.

But the world is round.
The further we walk
The closer we come
To the point of departure.
We scavenge along the way
Only enough for our own needs.
Nothing remains to put back,
Nothing to hand on.

There are cracks all over
The walls of city buildings.
The skin of a farmer
Who dries
And dies
Along with the crops,
The structure of a state
No longer able
To support itself.

We committed no sin
To cause this drought.
No sin, that is,
Of incest,
Rape,
Abuse of property,
Merely failed to respect
That which gave us life.

For Coral

by Romey Buchheit

A glint of anguish you murmured thin and fragile
In and out of my life.

As my next child bulged ungainly outward
Your photo, there on the wall,
   brown uptilting naked breasts
Soft eyes staring at my dripping teats
Reminding me of who you were
With the ring on your finger
With the spoken promise on your lips
Still smiling with the memory
Understanding what we both could never have.

I yearned for word of you, pictured you
In Italy, being one within one
My own selfless striving in a dead trio almost quartet
Procreating for its own sake
   for the love of a man knowing
(For the photo travelled from wall to wall
   getting younger
The older I got)
My edges tattered.

At my request one day it went from wall
  into a drawer.
It came back some time later
  when things were out of control.
It's still there
Lying
Alongside those carefree days he cares to cherish
Like bits of cobweb floating
Holding dreams aloft.

I saw you today in a cup of tea
Not believing my hand not shaking
A soft roundness in tender colours
Moonstone gleaming pastel woman
No less, no more than I.

LITERACY PROGRAMME

It is one of the objectives of Zimbabwe Women Writers
to promote literacy among women.
1994 sees the first ZWW training programme for literacy
workers.
For the semi-literate we have commenced programmes in
basic writing and reading and are in need of simple
books and writing materials.
We now have a mobile library and in 1993 Branches
throughout the country started their own libraries.
We welcome the donation of books and writing materials
and any helpful texts for these projects.
If you are able to help, please communicate with our Head
Office at 78 Kaguvi Street, PO Box Harare

Yesterday is Gone

by Primrose Sibare

'Why didn't you tell me?' His voice was almost a whisper.

'Because I didn't know how you'd feel,' I answered.

'Are you sure?' he asked as though what he was seeing did not convince him.

'Yes, I'm pregnant.'

Albert was stunned. He stepped back. For a long time he said nothing. I was silent too, sad, for I knew I had made a dreadful error. I could feel him withdrawing from me; could feel his anger, his disapproval and his suspicion.

'It's not mine,' he said at last.

'You know that's not true.' Bile rose in my throat.

'Then how did you trick me into . . .'

'There was no trickery, Albert. I thought you loved me.'

He looked at me, not wanting to believe it, knowing it was true and I felt a terrible pain inside. I loved him still. I didn't want to love him. I wanted to hate him.

'What do you intend to do?' he asked.

'I have to ask you.'

'But you would have told me long ago if you knew it was mine.'

I could not have told him of my wonderful discovery. An odd sense of shyness flooded in me whenever I thought about it. What would he think? Would he be happy? Displeased? Indifferent? Even though we had been going out for a long time, I knew there were still barriers between us. The baby was a precious secret I hugged to myself, longing to tell him and yet . . .

'You have disappointed me,' he said, breaking into my thoughts.

He left. I knew that I had lost him. I watched him go and I felt dead inside. There was only one solution to my problem. I had to go away. I didn't belong here. I vowed I would make a place for myself and I would be somebody. I would show Albert.

It was then that I met Magret during this time of my depression. She told me her secret.

'Life goes on,' she said, 'coping, forging ahead. The weak ones give up and accept defeat. But the strong ones face facts for what they are and make the best of things.'

I looked at my new friend and knew what she said was true. She had had her share of sorrow and disappointment yet she managed to retain her vitality, her warmth, her strength and good humour. Yes, Magret was strong and she was a realist. I really did admire her for that.

I wished I could be like her . . .

Woman

by Barbara Makhalisa

Home is a hollow hovel
Vivacious offspring become disconsolate orphans
The fireplace stares and blinks cold ashes
The pots uncannily yawn and gape in stupor
Spirited summer mornings
Become sluggish winter nights
Frolicsome afternoons become melancholic and weepy
Fertile evenings become the desolate Kalahari
Peaceful sleep steals away, nightmares abound.

Woman
You are a gulp of cool water
On a sizzling day
You are the warm crackling fire
On a cold windy night
You are the brilliant torch
In an awesome haunt
You are a pillar and comfort
In weakness and distress

Rosey and Her Girls

by Ruth Gabi

Rosey graduated from college the same year as Rutendo. They were friends throughout their college years. Both stayed with their aunts—their father's sisters, so they had that in common. Apart from that, Rutendo liked Rosey because she was a cheerful girl. With her laughter, Rosey broke the monotonous routine of college life: of breakfast, lectures, lunch, lectures, supper and then library. Rosey always found something to laugh at and Rutendo, who was quiet by nature, also learned to laugh at the world and at herself.

Rutendo admired Rosey because she was fiercely independent. In their second year, Rosey declared: 'I will keep my hair natural. It's mine and I like it that way.' And she did—when all the girls on campus were straightening their hair with hot combs.

One day she laughed and said, 'If I feel like it, I might just decide not to get married.' Rutendo laughed too. It was natural for every woman to get married.

The year they graduated was the 'great dispersal'— so they called it. More than four hundred of them were scattered all over the country. Rosey was sent to a small town and her friend remained in the capital. After a year, Rosey's aunt told Rutendo that Rosey had a baby girl. Rutendo asked the obvious question,

'Is she married?'

"No.'

'Who is the father?'

'She won't say—and you know Rosey when she says she won't tell, that's it. All she says is, "It's my baby and I am going to keep her'."

Later that month, Rosey came to show her aunt the baby. Rutendo went too and admired the bouncing girl— who also had that familiar twinkle of laughter she had often seen in Rosey's eyes. Rosey was truly proud of her daughter and was very possessive.

Rutendo thought she would have better luck than Rosey's aunt and asked about her plans.

'What plans? I've already planned! I have a job and a baby. She is mine and I'm going to look after her and bring her up myself.'

'But,' asked Rutendo, 'aren't you going to get married to the father of the child?'

'Why should I!' retorted Rosey. 'I wanted a baby, and I have got one. The baby is mine and that is what is important.

She never revealed the name of the father.

After two years she appeared again from the small town with another baby and she gave them the same answers, but this time she told them of her plans: 'I want three children and hope the third one will be a boy so that the girls will have a brother.

The third child was a girl and Rosey said: 'Well, this is the end. It's me and my girls—and we'll make it!'

Rosey stayed in the small town and brought up three fiercely independent young women.

I Am Me

by Shilla Ndlovu

I am me
Do not try to re-arrange
I am happy with what I am
I will dance to nobody's tune.

Do not re-prepare me
Do not try to amend me—
I have no bends.

Do not try to beat me
I need no panel beating.
I won't change for conformity's sake.

Accept me the way I am
Or produce dust!

Drought

by Maureen Mataranyika

Crowding every centimetre of the borehole area
Men, women and children patiently wait—
Await for their turn for those few drops—
Few drops of cool precious water
That will quench their thirst and sustain life.
For, like a raging avenging spirit
The drought wages its war.

There is no more energy for emotion
There is no more strength to complain
Dark weary faces look expressionless.
This is drought, yes, in our land
Pouncing on us like a demented spirit.

Children with sagging skin, gray eyes, thin faces
No longer play in the sun or splash muddy water:
No longer jump up and down the hills.
Too weak to play, they wait for their next meal
A meal long ceased to be regular

The spirit medium, once a respected man,
Thought borehole water was a bad omen.
The school teacher, who never went to the well,
The healthworker who advised the need for clean water,
All dreadfully thin, scramble for the scarce water.

For how long are we going to sit and watch
Women with tiny little babies clutching at withered breasts
Breasts that no longer give milk?
Cattle die, people eat wild leaves in starvation
What will it be this time next year?
Can we stop the drought?
What can be done, Economist? Traditionalist?
Tell me, Christians!

ZWW HISTORY:

In our first year, 1990,
the following workshops were held:

Writing for Children—Jackie Collins
Radio Drama—Fiona Lloyd
Poetry—Christina Rungana
Manuscript Presentation—Barbara Nkala
Publishing—Judy Norton
Short Story Writing—Norma Kitson
Playwriting—Kathleen McCreary
Scriptwriting—Bertha Msora
The Novel—Lynne Reid Banks
Auto- and Biography—Norma Kitson
Unsafe Issues—Amanda Hammar
Politics of Women in Writing—N. Makamure
Images of Women in Writing—Ruth Weiss
Improving your Poetry—Michelle Baker
Improving your Prose—Fiona Lloyd

For Better or Worse

by Vee Ndlovu

Ruvimbo caught her husband's eyes across the examination couch. He quickly looked away and turned to gaze at the underweight frame of their youngest, the surprise child.

Their family had been complete eight years ago, or so they thought. It had taken time to adjust to the last few years. But Fungai quickly won all their hearts with his ready smile and bright eyes. He was thirteen months old now, but over the last few months he had lost his brightness, suffered from a cold which refused to go away, and now, the glands of his neck and throat seemed permanently swollen. Ndoga was now looking at the doctor's face, and Ruvimbo's gaze followed his.

Ellen had been both doctor and friend to Ruvimbo ever since she set up her practice not far from the university where Ndoga taught.

She told Fungai what a brave boy he was, 'As you know, Fungai has not been responding to the treatment I've been giving him. Last time he was here, we agreed that he should have a blood test. Well, I received the results yesterday. I'm afraid the test was positive for HIV . . .'

Ruvimbo looked down at the child sitting listlessly in her lap, and hugged him tight as her mind tried desperately to fix on something. If Fungai has HIV, she thought, the only place he could have got it was from me, and I could only have got it from . . .

113

Hot anger and despair flooded through her. She could feel a pressure building up inside her like a lava flow searching for a weak spot through which to burst, destroying everything in its path. She wanted to scream. She wanted to kill Ndoga, to leave him, to punish him for everything he had ever done to her, for the suffering of this poor child in her arms.

She relived the agony she had felt when she had met Maya—the sudden chilling knowledge that she and Ndoga were having an affair. Nothing in their relationship had prepared her for that. It was as though her entire being was slowly and painfully dissolving in bitter acid, while all around her family life continued as if nothing had happened. On the dressing table, beside the picture of their two children, stood his latest card. He was fond of extravagant declarations: 'You are my dream come true,' it said. He had signed with his usual flourish, adding, 'I will love you for ever.' That had been only a few short weeks ago, but now it seemed like years.

It was in ways like this that Ndoga had made her feel loved and secure . . . until she learned of his affair. In fact, only the depth of that security had stopped her from packing her bags, fetching Shungu from school, and running to her parents. But she couldn't run away. When their youngest daughter returned from nursery school, Ruvimbo sent her next door to play until supper, and by the time Ndoga returned from work, she had recovered some of her composure.

She could tell from his manner that he knew something was wrong, and so she looked at him clearly, 'You're having an affair with Maya!'

His eyes fell, and he came towards her, and put his hands on her shoulders. 'Yes,' he said, and looked into her eyes. 'You know I love you. You mean more to me than anyone else ever could. Maya is a good friend. We work together sometimes. . . It was just something that happened . . . I promise you that my relationship with her is no threat to my love for you. . .'

114

As his voice droned on, her heart froze over. She knew then that she was being faced with the riddle of 'The African Man', and that her expected response was to be 'the African wife': that these small lapses were something she should not concern herself with. As he went on in his reasonable tone, she wondered at her initial shock. For despite his education, his acquaintance with life in Europe, Ndoga had always retained that element of tradition. He was the Head-of-the-Family—the one who made the decisions. The fact that he usually did so on the basis of her advice did not remove the fact that those decisions were his to make.

It was the Head-of-the-Household who spoke to her now: the voice of wisdom; protector and defender. Why should she be surprised that he now demanded this other traditional African right? And knowing him so well, she knew too that this could not be argued with. Ndoga would not listen to her protests. The thing had nothing to do with her. It presented no threat. It would take nothing away from her. As he saw it.

As if she were far away, Ruvimbo heard a voice inside her head telling her that this was true. If Maya, or any other woman demanded more than he was willing to give, Ndoga would quickly write her off, but he would never give up his family. So she resigned herself, as he held her and stroked her, and then led her to the bedroom, where he made tender and passionate love to her. And life went on.

After a while, she realised that the affair with Maya had ended, and Ruvimbo pushed the issues of faith and fidelity to the back of her mind. Later, she tried to talk to him about it, to explain how it hurt her; to try and understand what it was that made him do it. He explained that he would never keep it secret from her, but neither would he go out of his way to tell her about it. She was his only wife in the eyes of the world, the mother of his children, and he respected her more than any other person. She must try to understand him. Her only recourse was to accept, and to make sure that he continued to respect her above all others.

All these thoughts rushed through her mind as she sat in the surgery, and their friend talked about Fungai. Ruvimbo had never dreamed that his affairs could destroy them. She never thought that AIDS would strike their family. Suddenly her life was a nightmare from which there could be no waking up.

Ellen was speaking, but Ruvimbo could not hear her. She caught sight of Ndoga's stricken face, and suddenly she could bear it no more. She stood up. 'Excuse me. I, I have to go—'

She walked blindly through the streets, holding Fungai so tightly that he cried out, and she could hold back her tears no longer. Her mind could only repeat, Oh God, Oh God, like a scratched record. . . no longer useful, damaged, condemned—.

Sitting in a secluded corner of the park, she thought with a start of guilt how she had felt when she became pregnant with Fungai. She had not wanted to be tied down again to the routine of baby care. Was this her punishment for wishing a miscarriage? But as soon as she thought it, she dismissed it. From the minute she first saw Fungai she loved him completely. What would happen to them all, she wondered, and what of this poor sweet child nestled in her lap? Was he to suffer, never to grow up because of Ndoga's weakness and selfishness? Her thoughts shifted to him. Would she, could she, stay with him?

She hated him for this: that he had not listened to her, that he had only seen his own desires. If only she had been stronger. At least she should have insisted that they use condoms.

The driveway was empty. She wondered blankly where Nodga had gone, what he might be going through. Then as she closed the door, the telephone began to ring.

'Yes?' she said reluctantly, as she lifted the receiver.

'Ruvimbo, thank God you're home! I was beginning to get really worried.' It was Ellen.

'Listen,' she went on. 'Maidei is on her way over there now to pick up the children and take them to my mother's for supper. I'm must finish up at the surgery, and then I'll be straight over. Just get out the brandy and wait for me. Okay?'

'Okay,' said Ruvimbo, overwhelmed with relief that someone else had taken over, that she would not have to pretend that things were all right while her world was collapsing around her. 'By the way,' continued Ellen, 'don't worry about Ndoga. I called Godfrey. He's at our house now. I'll be with you soon.'

Godfrey was Ndoga's brother, and Ellen's husband. Ruvimbo had introduced them and they had married five years before. Godfrey knew of Ndoga's affairs, and though he had not condoned them, he was probably the only person to whom Ndoga would feel able to talk.

She put the phone down just as Maidei drove up. A few minutes later the children bounded into the room and out again, Maidei holding the baby. Ruvimbo waved them off at the gate, thankful that they had been too excited to notice how quiet she was.

She went indoors to wait for Ellen. Her mind turned to Ndoga, and the bitterness welled up again. She would not try to lighten his burden this time. She wasn't even sure she could cope with her own. How she wished she could just run away, but whatever she did, wherever she went, the horror would be with her. Nothing she could do would make it go away. Acknowledging that somehow seemed to calm her. Perhaps it was the effect of the brandy.

She wondered how Ndoga must be feeling—he who held the family as a sacred thing—to know that he had set his own on a path of certain destruction through his weakness and selfishness. A part of her pitied him, but she had no sympathy for him. Let Godfrey comfort him. She must make her own decisions before she could think of her husband. How much time did they have left, she and Ndoga, before their family was torn apart, their children orphaned?

She heard Ellen's car pull into the drive. As they greeted each other, silently, each saw the same sorrow and fear reflected in the other's face. They embraced, and made their way to the living room.

Ellen spoke of her own feelings of guilt: that she hadn't warned Ndoga about the new dangers in behaving as he did; that she hadn't thought to warn Ruvimbo; that she hadn't said plainly that whatever they might decide, Ndoga must use condoms. But he was an intelligent man. He read the newspapers. Why hadn't he taken precautions? She was exhausted too by the possibilities, the inevitability of the tragedy about to overcome this family which she loved as her own.

They talked for a long time, mostly about Fungai, and what they should tell the other children and the grandparents. He had at the most, Ellen felt, a few months before he succumbed completely to one of the infections assaulting his body. All they could do was to make sure that he suffered as little as possible.

There could be no question of another child. Ellen explained that pregnancy seemed to weaken the body's resistance to the virus, and it could further endanger Ruvimbo's health. And eventually they talked about Ruvimbo and Ndoga, and what was going to happen to them. The false reality created by the brandy's warm glow allowed Ruvimbo to talk about it as though it were happening to someone else.

'People sometimes live for years with the virus before they show any signs of illness, Ruvimbo. Medical science knows so little about it yet. They can't even be certain that everyone who is infected with HIV will develop AIDS. After all,' she said, appealing to her friend's common sense, 'what other disease has had a one hundred percent success rate? The Black Death in Britain killed a lot of people, but some survivied. Why shouldn't you be the exception that proves the rule?'

Ruvimbo looked at her doubtfully.

'You have to hold onto that idea. One thing I am

118

sure about. You must believe that you can combat this. If you don't, then your body will give up too. And you must also try, as far as possible, to avoid situations you find stressful. You must follow a healthy lifestyle, and eat plenty of good, fresh food.'

This was all the advice that Ellen, even as a doctor, could offer her friend.

'So what do you want Ruvimbo? Do you want Ndoga to stay, or would you rather he went away for a while to give you some time to think?'

Ruvimbo wondered whether Ndoga would want to come back. Neither woman was under any illusion about the depth of the guilt and self-punishment he must be going through.

Suddenly Ruvimbo realised that Ndoga must also wish that he could run away, even more desperately than she. The thought took hold that she could not bear for them to be apart. They had shared joy and pain alike for the last fifteen years, rarely spending more than a few days apart. How could they be alone now when each needed strength and support more than ever?

She must see him. She would not let him run away from them and from his responsibilities. This time there would be no concessions. Ndoga would do as she wanted; she would make him. He owed her and the children that much.

At half past seven they called Ellen's house. Ruvimbo's mouth was dry as she heard Ellen ask Godfrey: 'Is he ready to come home?'

A lengthy conversation followed, but finally Ellen agreed that she and Ruvimbo would go there. Godfrey could promise nothing. Ndoga seemed to be in a state of shock.

Minutes later, they pulled up in Ellen's driveway. Immediately, Ruvimbo got out and walked up the front steps. The door opened and Ndoga stood there, tears streaming down his face. Ruvimbo walked towards him, her arms held open, and together they went into the house.

The Me the World Doesn't See

by Tawona Mtshiya

If I could climb the highest mountain,
I could let the whole world know my secret.

Time is just not on my side.
By the time I get my outward bound equipment
To head for the mountain—
Morning is over.

By the time I want to mobilise
Those who understand my language
It's already lunchtime—
No one is willing to listen
Except to worry about their stomachs.

By the time I want to push everyone
To head for the mountain—
It's 5 pm—
Time to fight for transport at the bus depot.

Night time viciously creeps in.
Still—
The world hasn't seen me.

Why?

?

by Chiramwiwa Lato

Round and round I go
Back and forth—I never stop
But I still come to the same place—
To the same beginning.

Like a tick, I cling to the idea
That someday I will make it:
I will put everything on paper
I will paint my face with words
And people will see and be amazed and puzzled
They'll see a face within a face
That face will show love, pain, hope—
Dreams fulfilled, and unfulfilled
In those words will be a face
Telling of many happenings
For words are the door to my inner being—
The real me.
What exists outside is just a front
To guard against the too cold cruel weather.

Round and round I go
Back and forth—I never stop
But I still come to the same place
To the same beginning
That is my face,
Within my heart.

AIDS

by Mrs S.E. Makasi

Let's give the victims love
But not make love.
Let's not starve them
But mercifully care
And feed them.

Let's not curse them
But heartily pray for them
And for ourselves
For no one knows
What fate has in store for us.

AIDS is like a bullet
One is either missed or shot dead.
Its various ways of spreading
Are now difficult to understand.

Let's pray to God
He delivered the Israelites
After forty years of slavery
He too cannot allow us
To be victims forever.

Our commitment is to pray
To spread the news
But not the disease.

Going Home

by Ruth Gabi

Nyasha could not postpone the journey any longer. She had to go. For a whole month now she had been worrying about her mother in the village. In January she had been unable to go home because all her money had gone on school fees. Now it was getting to the end of February and she really had to go—alone. She could already see her mother's disappointed face asking, 'You left the children?' If she took all the children she would not be able to take her mother enough provisions and anyway it was too expensive. Travelling from Harare to Sanyati with three children was also tiring.

She wondered what her mother was living on—what with this terrible drought! She, Nyasha, was the only one who was supporting her mother since she was divorced years ago when Nyasha was still a child. Her three other sisters were married and, like her mother, were living off the land.

Her mother was a sensible woman. When she divorced, she had gone back to her home area in Sanyati. There she had been allocated a field and, by her standards, had become quite a successful cotton farmer on her own. In the past Nyasha helped her mother only now and then as her mother was able to get enough to support herself from the cotton she grew. But this year was different. Never had a drought so devastating struck the land. Even people in towns were suffering: they who are not normally affected by drought.

On the bus, Nyasha thought of the maize in her back garden. It depressed her. The year before they had a bumper harvest. The whole family used to tease Ticha, her three year old son, not to wander into the maize patch in case he got lost. This year the maize stalks were very thin and sickly and crying out for rain. If things were that bad in town then it must be worse in Sanyati.

It was. She got to hear of it on the Sanyati-bound bus. The bus going to the rural areas was noisier because most of the people knew each other. It was a pleasant atmosphere and Nyasha felt relaxed. The Saturday early morning bus she got from Harare to Kadoma had been too quiet for comfort. The Sanyati bus, however, was bubbling with life as friends and relatives exchanged news. Nyasha got a seat near the back. As she sat down, a thin wiry man passed her saying loudly to no one in particular: 'I want to sit at the back. That is where there's lots of news'.

'Yes, come!' cried a man who was already sitting there and they immediately got into conversation.

The bus left Kadoma and on entering the farming area, the talk inevitably turned to the drought-stricken land. The jovial mood died down. The stark reality of how desperate the land was, was only too visible. All eyes were glued to the windows as they viewed the wilted maize in the fields and the cotton which was less than half a metre in height. Cotton, a crop which usually grew to about a metre in height in a good season, looked very pathetic.

Many people shook their heads silently. The silence was broken by the thin man sitting at the back who said: 'Ah, you shake your heads at this? This is nothing! You haven't seen anything yet! You wait and see when we get to the resettlement area. There, the cotton even refused to form balls!'

'Eh, comrade,' responded his neighbour in a faded blue safari suit, 'it makes you wonder what we did wrong'.

'Friends, too many sins have been committed. The soil is saturated with blood. Some of our sons and daughters from the war have not yet been buried,' said an elderly

124

man chewing away at some sugar cane. 'But some sins being committed now are so abominable that even he, the Almighty, must be disgusted. Did you hear what happened in town recently?'

'No!' What happened?' responded a number of people at the back.

'One man made his own daughter his wife!' said the thin man triumphantly.

'What?' exclaimed the listeners.

'Yes, his own daughter!' repeated the thin man. 'A beautiful girl who was doing Form Four at secondary school, and now she has given birth to a baby girl fathered by her own father. Now tell me, what will that child call the man? Father, or grandfather?'

'That is clearly a difficult case,' said a man in a green jacket. 'But where was his wife when all this was happening?'

'With him. And she is the one who went to report to the police that she had been chased away and that her husband had made their daughter pregnant. Now comrades, with such crimes being committed, do you think the rains will fall?' asked the thin man.

'Oh, it is terrible when a chicken eats its own eggs,' was all one of the listeners could conclude.

Suddenly the driver hooted. There was a goat on the road some distance away. The driver felt it best to get it off the road long before he got to that point. There was already enough misery without adding any more by killing some communal farmer's remaining goat.

There was silence again on the bus as it had now left the resettlement area and had entered the communal areas. A lump rose in Nyasha's throat. The houses looked so desolate and the state of the fields was enough to make her swallow hard. The cotton was so short that even if the rains came, it would not revive it.

The villagers sat in the shade of their huts. From the state of the maize Nyasha could see that that year they would not taste green maize. The stalks of the short maize plants were bent double, touching the scorched earth. When nature calls the tips of the maize plant back to the soil, that is disaster, she thought. She was yet to see her mother's fields.

Nyasha could see that everyone was groping for an answer to the disaster and that these people were trying to make sense of their plight. She wondered if they would understand all this talk about the depletion of the ozone layer and how they should all be involved in the fight to save planet earth. Education will have to start soon before more damage is done. She was glad the schools had started educating children about the importance of preserving the vegetation.

A few weeks before, her eight-year-old daughter, Vari, had come with homework on the environment. She kept asking everybody in the house why trees were important. Nyasha smiled as she remembered her daughter cutting pictures from newspapers and magazines and pasting them in her book. Vari was a true disciple for preserving planet earth. She had taken it upon herself to educate her young brother and sister. So well had she educated them that one day Nyasha was amused to hear Ticha singing: 'Pollution! Pollution!' at the top of his voice. Later, Vari asked her, 'Do people who smoke pollute the air?'. 'Yes, they do.' Nyasha replied, 'Then I will tell Sekuru to stop smoking when I see him,' said Vari with determination. Nyasha smiled in admiration. She knew her daughter would tell her grandfather just that, and then proceed to give him a lecture on pollution. All that she had learned at school would be poured out on him—the plea from the children not to kill the world.

Nyasha got off at the growth point and began the long walk to her mother's village. She dreaded this part of the journey because there was no proper road. There was a footpath which disappeared now and then into the gulleys. When you asked the villagers where the path was, they pointed among the trees and said: 'Oh, there it is, near that baobab tree and then you turn left when you get to a homestead with a fence. That is the path that leads to Chimuti village.'

With the bag of provisions firmly on her head, she set off. There were many deep gulleys on the side of the path. Nyasha wondered how people managed to travel along that path at night. She trudged on through cotton fields. At close range the cotton plants looked even more miserable. Some of the plants were just a few centimetres high. She passed a maize field where the stalks were bent double. The maize had tasselled before it even got to waist level. Some of the dry plants whose tassels were on the ground were already being eaten by termites.

Next to the maize field was a small area where there were groundnuts. There was no hope of the groundnuts reviving at all. The leaves were burnt brown by the sun but the owner had still carefully weeded the field and even put extra soil around each plant, hoping, just hoping for a miracle from the great heavens.

After walking for about an hour, she got to Chimuti river. It was now just a river by name because no water had flowed in it for some time. That it had been a river to reckon with in the past was evident from the trees that hung precariously way above the river bed. Now, Nyasha's feet sank into the hot river sand and she looked for areas where big stones jutted out from the river bed so that she could use them as stepping stones.

She arrived at her mother's home as the sun was setting. The first one to see her as she entered her mother's cotton field was Shamiso, her deaf and dumb niece. She ran through the field and grabbed the bag from her. Shamiso made happy gurgling sounds. Nyasha smiled and shook her hand. She stretched her arms. The travelling bag had dug deep into her shoulders.

Her mother's cotton field was no different from the ones she had already seen. Her mother stood up from under the shade of the house. She was wearing a brown dress. 'Eh! Eh! Welcome,' she cackled. 'You are alone?' Nyasha smiled. She would explain later.

'It is as if I knew you were coming,' her mother continued, without waiting for an answer. 'I was supposed to go to a church meeting this afternoon. I was just feeling weak the whole day so I didn't go. Ah, it is good you have come! Here in the village there is nothing good. God seems to have forgotten us this year, but we will continue praying.'

Shamiso gave her some water to drink and then Nyasha was pleasantly surprised when her mother emerged from the hut with a huge watermelon.

'What! You mean, in spite of the drought you have managed to harvest that from the field?'

'Yes,' her mother replied. 'I planted them with the first rains and by the time the rains disappeared in late January, they were almost ready'.

'Hmm, it is really delicious,' said Nyasha as she dug her teeth into the chunks of the watermelon.

'Yes, they are,' said her mother. 'They are the only things we have eaten this season from the field. It would have been better if I had made peanut butter with the groundnuts I wasted in that field'. 'She pointed at the dry plants not far off, close to the cotton field.

'Yes, I can see,' agreed Nyasha. Her mother's cotton field came to within a metre of the house. The few cotton plants that had cotton balls on them were very short. 'This year you will have to bend very low to harvest,' joked Nyasha, attempting to lift her mother's spirits.

She remembered the times when she had helped her mother harvest cotton in the past. There had been no need to bend then. The cotton stalks were tall and strong. 'If I manage to harvest half a bale of cotton from this field this year I will be very lucky,' said her mother. 'The situation is very bad. Some people around here will not harvest anything at all. We will all have to depend on drought relief. I hope they start bringing the maize soon. Nobody eats food outside any longer like they used to. There are too many hungry people wandering around.'

Nyasha and her mother talked long into that night near the dying fire as they exchanged news from town and country. Above them the sky was ablaze with stars and the moon was full.

'You know my neighbour Mbuya Themba is grief-stricken,' said her mother. 'Her eldest son, Themba, who was working in Shurugwi collapsed at work and died. He is the one who built the house she is living in now and he was supporting her. Her youngest son, Fanuel, who stays with her is no good and married when he was still very young. All they do, him and his wife, is trouble Mbuya Themba. At the funeral I think she lost her head and said: "God, you should have taken this loafer Fanuel." Fanuel was not amused at all.' They both laughed.

Nyasha gave her mother letters her children had written. 'Ei, Ei,' said her mother, clapping her hands with happiness.' I will show the women at church the letters from my grandchildren.'

The next morning after breakfast, Nyasha prepared for the journey back to Harare. The sky was very clear—too clear for comfort. There was not a cloud in the sky at a time when they should have been rumbling, pregnant with rain. At 10 o'clock when Nyasha was leaving, the heat was already unbearable.

'Shamiso will walk you to Baba Nhamo's house and then you can team up with him. He is going back to Kadoma today where he teaches. He usually comes at weekends to check on his field. Thank you for coming. I will see you in May,' her mother said.

'Yes, do come when you have finished clearing the fields. Goodbye.'

Shamiso took her bag and led the way through the cotton field. Nyasha looked back. Her mother was still standing in the cotton field with its stunted crop. She stood there looking upwards to the heavens as if making a silent prayer for the parched land. She knew that the death of the land meant death for all.

Hope lay with the new generation—the children of today who will inherit a sick earth—an earth that needs a lot of care in order to survive.

It Is Mine?

by Colette Mutangadura

So beautiful and wonderful
So lovely to hold against me
So sweetly scented a creature
Is it mine?

What a change this has brought to me
What a loving heart I feel inside me
What attentiveness it has awakened in me
Is it really Mine?

I hold the body closely and admire
I spend endless hours staring into the eyes
I feel so much for this little creature
Is it mine?

I have received this precious gift
I'm so happy I don't know what to say.
Tears fall and I can't help it
Is it really mine?

This first seed of mine stares at me
My eyes look down upon it
I have received what I longed to have
A baby of my own.

Of Fathers

by Megan Allardice

Thinking of fathers
Yours,
Mine,
Sylvia Plath's

Yours,
A passionate relationship,
So you can say
You come
From a family of passion.
No guts to say
'No'
And yet
He does not send
The money
You so desperately need.

Mine,
On one third my income
Presses notes into my hand,
Wishes
To buy me lunch
Or dinner.
But passion?
No.
Love?
A little.

It is a rare
And expensive commodity
Though much in need.

And Plath's?
A 'bastard'
A bastard in his absence,
Because of his absence.
He left her
And left her always
With the fear
Of others also leaving.
His death a desertion,
She searched for him
In mother, lover, husband, son,
Finally in herself,
And
When she could not replace him,
Killed him anew
With her words.

I have never called
My father a bastard.
What would it prove?
I would,
Inevitably,
Be forgiven,
The alternative being
Loss
Of my apparent
Love.

You
Have done
I'm sure.
Perhaps you model yourself on Sylvia,
Model your 'Daddy'
On her bastard.

But you are
Well past
Your thirtieth year
And still fighting.
You conceded
Recently
You are not suicidal.

But Plath?
Had a dead father to reach.
Attempted to reach him
Through death,
Envied his choice,
Envied his attaining,
Effortlessly,
That finality.

And what now
Of the three of us?
Sylvia and Daddy
United in death.
Did he measure up
To her eight-year-old
Untainted image?
And you and me,
Still running.
You blindly,
With blind hope
Toward your father.

I
Needing to grow,
Needing to escape my child role,
No longer feigning daughterlove
Am running away.

I Am Growing Up

by Lizzie Mamvura

I am growing up
And people think I will never go away
That I will always live with you
Be washed and dressed by you
Even at the age of twenty

The perfect offspring who never leaves the nest.

You teach me to be independent
A strong individual
To have my own opinions
To earn my own living
Neither of us knows
If one day—only one day—I will wash and dress
            myself
And live independently.

But I haven't been programmed to be anybody's wife
Lover
Or mother.
You didn't teach me to serve anybody
To wash or peel potatoes.

People appreciate my intelligence
My wit and creativity
Sharpness and humour.
You call me 'Mai veCock!'
Refusing to innoculate me against rubella
You ignore my sexuality.

The Girl Who Can

by Ama Ata Aidoo

They say that I was born in Hasodzi; and it is a big village in the Central Region of our country, Ghana. They also say that when all of Africa is not choking under a drought, Hasodzi lies in a very fertile low land in a district that is known for its good soil. Maybe that is why any time I don't finish eating my food, Nana says, 'You, Adjoa, you don't know what life is about—you don't know what problems there are in this life . . .'

As far as I could see, there was only one problem. And it had nothing to do with what I knew Nana considered as 'problems', or what Maami thinks of as 'the problem'.

Maami is my mother. Nana is my mother's mother. And they say I am seven years old. And my problem is that at this seven years of age, there are things I can think in my head, but which, maybe, I do not have the proper language to speak them out with. And that, I think, is a very serious problem.

Because it is always difficult to decide whether to keep quiet and not say anything of the things that come into my head, or say them and get laughed at. Not that it is easy to get any grown-up to listen to you even when you decide to take the risk and say something serious to them.

Take Nana. First, I have to struggle to catch her attention. Then I tell her something I have taken a long time to figure out. And then you know what always happens? She at once stops whatever she is doing, stares at me for a very long time. Then, bending and turning her head slightly so that one of her ears comes down towards

135

me, she'll say in that voice: 'Adjoa, you say what?' After I have repeated whatever it was I had said, she would either—still in that voice—ask me 'never, never, but NEVER to repeat THAT,' or she would immediately burst out laughing. She would laugh and laugh, until tears ran down her cheeks and she stopped whatever she was doing and wiped away the tears with the hanging edges of her cloth. And she would continue laughing until she was completely tired. But then, as soon as another person comes by, just to make sure she doesn't forget whatever it was I had said, she would repeat it to her. And then, of course, there are three, four or even more of such laughing and screaming tear-faced grown-ups. And all that performance because of whatever I'd said?

I find something quite confusing in all this. That is, no one ever explains to me why sometimes I shouldn't repeat some things I say, while other times, some other things I say would not only be all right, but would be considered so funny, they would be repeated so many times for so many people's enjoyment. You see now neither way of hearing me out can encourage me to express my thoughts too often?

Like all this business to do with my legs. I have always wanted to tell them not to worry. I mean Nana and my mother. That it did not have to be an issue for my two favourite people to fight over. But I didn't want either to be told not to repeat that or for it to be considered so funny that they would laugh at me until they cried. After all, they were my legs . . .

When I think back on it now, those two—Nana and my mother—must have been discussing my legs from the day I was born. What I am sure of is that when I came out of the land of sweet soft silence into the world of noise and comprehension, the first topic I met was my legs.

That discussion was repeated regularly.

Nana: 'Ah, ah, you know, I thank my God that your very first child is female. But Kaya, I'm not sure about her legs. Hm . . . hm . . . hm . . .' And Nana would shake her head.

Maami: 'Mother, why are you always complaining about Adjoa's legs? If you ask me . . .'

Nana: 'They are too thin. And I'm not asking you! Nana has many voices. There is a special one she uses to shut everyone up.

'Some people have no legs at all,' my mother would try again with all her small courage.

'But Adjoa has legs,' Nana would insist, 'except that they are too thin. And also too long for a woman. Kaya, listen. Once in a while, but only once in a very long while, somebody decides nature, a child's spirit mother, an accident happens, and somebody gets born without arms or legs or both sets of limbs. And then, let me touch wood, it is a sad business. And you know, such things are not for talking about every day. But if any female child decides to come into this world with legs, then they might as well be legs.'

'What kind of legs?'

And always at that point, I knew from her voice that my mother was weeping inside herself. Nana never heard such inside weeping. Not that it would have stopped Nana even if she heard it, which always surprised, me, because, about almost everything else apart from my legs, Nana is such a good grown-up.

In any case, what do I know about good grown-ups and bad grown-ups? How could Nana be a good grown-up when she carried on so about my legs? All I want to say is that I really liked Nana except for that.

Nana: 'As I keep saying, if any woman decides to come into this world with all of her two legs, then she should select legs that have meat on them: with good calves, because you are sure such legs would support solid hips. And a woman must have solid hips to be able to have children.'

'Oh, Mother!' That's how my mother would answer. Very very quietly. And the discussion would end or they would move on to something else.

Sometimes, Nana would pull in something about

my father. How, 'Looking at such a man, we have to be humble and admit that after all, God's children are many . . .' How, 'After one's only daughter had insisted on marrying a man like that, you still have to thank your God that the biggest problem you got later was having a granddaughter with spindly legs that are too long for a woman and too thin to be of any use . . .'

The way she always added that bit about my father under her breath, she probably thought I didn't hear it. But I always heard it. Plus, that is what always shut my mother up for good. So that even if I had not actually heard the words, once my mother looked like even her little courage was finished, I could always guess what Nana had added to the argument.

'Legs that have meat on them with good calves to support solid hips . . . to be able to have children'

So I wished that one day I would see, for myself, the legs of any woman who had children. But in our village, that is not easy. The older women wear long wrap-arounds all the time. Perhaps if they let me go bathe in the river in the evening, I could have checked. But I never had the chance. It took a lot of begging just to get my mother and Nana to let me go splash around in the shallow end of the river with my friends, who were other little girls like me. For proper baths, we used the small bathhouse behind our hut. Therefore, the only naked female legs I have ever really seen are those of other little girls like me, or older girls in the school. And those of my mother and Nana: two pairs of legs which must surely belong to the approved kind: because Nana gave birth to my mother and my mother gave birth to me. In my eyes all my friends have got legs that look like legs: but whether the legs have got meat on them to support the kind of hips that . . . that I don't know.

According to the older boys and girls, the distance between our village and the small town is about five kilometres. They always complain about how long it is to walk to school and back. But to me, we live in our village, and walking those kilometres doesn't matter. School is nice.

School is another thing Nana and my mother discussed often and appeared to have different ideas about. Nana thought it would be a waste of time. I never understood what she meant. My mother seemed to know, and disagreed. She kept telling Nana that she, that is, my mother, felt that she was locked into some kind of darkness because she didn't go to school. So that if I, her daughter, could learn to write and read my own name and a little besides—perhaps be able to calculate some things on paper—that would be good. I could always marry and maybe . . .

Nana would just laugh. 'Ah, maybe with legs like hers, she might as well go to school.'

Running with our classmates on our small sports field and winning first place each time never seemed to me to be anything about which to tell anyone at home.

This afternoon was different. I don't know how the teachers decided to let me run for the junior section of our school in the district games. But they did.

When I went home to tell my mother and Nana, they had not believed it at first. So Nana had taken it upon herself to go and 'ask into it properly'. She came home to tell my mother that it was really true. I was to be one of my school's runners.

'Is that so?' exclaimed my mother. I know her. Her mouth moved as though she was going to tell Nana, that, after all, there was a secret about me she couldn't be expected to share with anyone. But then Nana looked so pleased that out of surprise, my mother shut her mouth up. In any case, since the first time they heard the news, I have often caught Nana staring at my legs with a strange look on her face, but still pretending like she was not looking.

All this week, she has been washing my school unifrom herself. That is a big surprise. And she didn't stop at that. She even went to Mr Mensah's house and borrowed

139

his charcoal pressing iron, each time, came back home with it, and ironed and ironed and ironed the uniform. Until, if I had been the uniform, I would have said aloud that I had had enough.

Wearing my school uniform this week has been very nice. At the parade the first afternoon, it caught the rays of the sun and shone brighter than everybody else's uniform. I'm sure Nana saw that too, and must have liked it.

Yes, she has been coming into town with us every afternoon of this district sports week. Each afternoon, she has pulled one set of fresh old cloth from the big brass bowl to wear. And those old cloths are always so stiffly starched, you can hear the cloth creak when she passed by. But she walks way behind us school children. As though she was on her own way, some place else.

Yes, I have won every race I ran in for my school. And I have won the cup for the best all-round junior athlete.

Yes, Nana said that she didn't care if such things are not done. She would do them. You know what she did? She carried the gleaming cup on her back, like they do with babies. And other very precious things. And this time, not taking the trouble to walk by herself.

When we arrived in our village, she entered our compound to show the cup to my mother before going to give it back to the Headmaster.

Oh, grown-ups are so strange. Nana is right now carrying me on her knee, and crying softly. Muttering, muttering, muttering. That 'Saa, thin legs can also be useful . . . thin legs can also be useful . . .' That 'even though some legs don't have much meat on them, to carry hips . . ., they can run. Thin legs can run . . . And then, who knows? . . .'

I don't know too much about such things. But that's how I was feeling and thinking all along. That surely one should be able to do other things with legs besides having them to support hips that can make babies. Except that I

140

was afraid of saying that sort of thing aloud, because someone would have told me never, never, but NEVER to repeat such words. Or else, they would have laughed so much at what I'd said, they would have cried.

It's much better this way. Acted out. To show them. Although I could not have planned it.

As for my mother, she has been speechless.

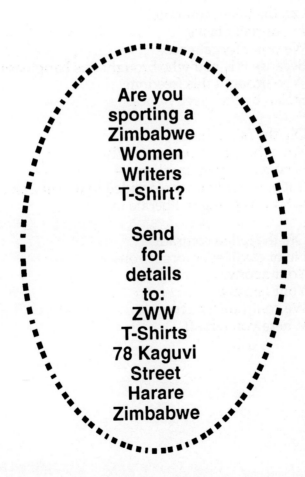

Fallen Comrade

by Spelile Shereni

Oh, the fallen comrade!
In our daily tasks
We don't forget you
Because it is you who brought this happiness
Who brought this freedom
Stolen by the greedy ones.

Oh, the fallen hero!
You who gave up your family
Who gave up your village—
If it was not you who decided to live like an animal
Who was going to liberate us?

Oh, the fallen comrade
No one will ever forget you—
Your agony,
Your last cry
We continue the struggle
Where you left off.

Love

by Rosemary Smith-Kebe

Have you ever been enchanted by a sun-drenched
    morning?
When the sunlight reaches into every corner of the
    garden
and into every room in the house?

Everything stands out clearly: colours, objects
flowers, old books and
dust-covered cupboards.

Outside, each blade of grass exists
apart, clearly outlined
and sheds its tiny shadow proudly.

Here, inside,
tiny particles dance in the light-filled air.
Dust-dust
stardust
dream-dust
Death dust come once again alive
re-vitalised by sunlight

A bit of this sunlight enters my soul.
It lightens up memories and yet unanswered dreams.
It lights up hope which always lingers
And long-forgotten corners of myself.

Yesterday shouldn't have happened

by Hilary Homans

As she woke she knew something terrible was wrong.
To comfort herself she found the edge of the bed
and gripped it tightly.
Then slowly easing her grasp
she opened her eyes.
Everything looked the same;
the sun beating in through the dark, heavy curtains;
the birds singing their unceasing songs.

But something was different.
She tried to remember.
Then slowly she realised what it was.
Yesterday was no ordinary day
Yesterday war had broken out.

A wave of panic overtook her
and she rushed to draw back the curtains
and everything looked the same;
the radiant sky;
the quality of light;
the quantity of bird life.
None of this was diminished, or as yet destroyed,
here at least.

'Best listen to the radio
for the latest information,' she thought.
Male, cold, detached voices droning on
in their best BBC cultivated English
about sorties, strategies, missions and targets.

No mention of people, lives lost,
destruction and devastation.

Is this the result of all those coffee table games
like 'Risk; and 'Battleships' these men were weaned on?
They learned the language of war in their infancy,
but never experienced the *reality*.
Now, as adults, they think it is all a game.
You place a mark on a map, your target,
Then attack at a precise moment.
End of sorties,
but not end of war.

Now here's a different voice.
Not the usual detached, strategic tone,
but one which talks of the star-spangled missiles
being showered on Baghdad.
Is this for real?
Is he waxing romantically and eloquently on missiles
as if they were shooting stars falling from the galaxy?

This is too much.
Off goes the radio.
The anger wells up inside and
She is tempted to throw the machine through the window,
But that would be to resort to the same tactics.
By ignoring the radio she would be pretending
that the reality does not exist.
Shying away from the bloodshed, grief,
annihilation and violation of living beings.

As a woman she knows all about violation,
but her response is not one of surrender and submission.
So she calms herself and shouts
This has to STOP!

Pregnancy

by Colette Mutangadura

Early morning sickness wakes me up
Spitting and vomiting like an angry cobra.
My character is becoming moody and shrewish.
I cannot help this situation.

My whole body is changing—into what?
I wonder if others notice me change
I look into the mirror and get a shock—
Surprised at the figure I see staring at me.

My eyes are pale with a lazy look,
My neck stretched out like a peacock's
My tummy is a great balloon bulging out,
My chest, in size, has doubly increased.

I crave for one thing and dislike another.
I like some people and hate the sight of others
I am clumsy—so clumsy!—I can't help it,
Sleepy and yawning during all the days.

Everyone fusses over me
As if I can no longer fend for myself!
But I live a life full of caution and care
For my unborn baby—and myself.

Love was meant for me

by Dorah Kamanga

I stood on my toes to get a good look at the man who was talking. The Secretary of Education had come to address the crowd of striking teachers who had gathered outside the education offices.

'The Government has heard your demands. They will act on them soon enough,' he said. But the roar of the teachers was deafening as they opposed his statement.

I don't know what got into me. I found myself shouting obscenities at him at the top of my voice.

One event led to another. One over-zealous man started it all. He sent a missile hurtling towards the Secretary. The angry crowd surged forward. On seeing the explosive situation developing, the riot squad fired tear gas canisters. All hell broke loose!

I took out my handkerchief and put it over my mouth. Then I turned and fled. Screams rent the air which was full of white stinging smoke. As the teachers ran, they overturned cars and broke shop windows. More police were called to reinforce the already battling forces.

As I rounded a corner into one of the busiest streets in town, a baton-wielding policeman confronted me. I had picked up a brick and sent it whistling through the air. I missed my target. The policeman attacked. I heard myself scream. My knees felt weak. I began to go down and felt a strong pair of arms reach out for me before I hit the ground.

'Hurry! Follow me.' The owner of the hands beckoned me as he led me into an alley. I followed, limping on weak legs.

When we were safe from the screams, the teargas and the fighting the man turned to look at me.

147

'Lady, you sure can fight! Are you okay?'

I touched the spot where the baton had hit me. My forehead had a nasty bump. 'Apart from this bump and an awful headache, I think I'm all right,' I said.

'My apartment is just around the corner. Come with me and I'll put something on that head of yours.'

I found myself warming to this tall, handsome, dark stranger who had saved me from serious injury.

In his apartment, he made me comfortable while he busied himself warming up water and applying an antiseptic to my poor head. In a few minutes I began to feel much better. I marvelled at the gentleness of his big hands. Now that I had the chance to be close to him, I discovered that he was not only handsome, he was also kind and charming—just like Bill, I thought. A twinge of pain ran through me as I thought of Bill.

Bill and I had been in love for over two years. We were planning to marry in December the previous year when, in the blinding rain, his car left the road and hit a lamp post. He was killed instantly.

For two years, I hadn't thought of love. Perhaps with Bill's death, love was not meant for me. Bill had been everything that I ever lived for. He was understanding, loving and kind. Only Bill had made me feel like a woman.

Recently, I had managed to pull myself together a little and was slowly pushing the haunting memories of Bill to the back of my mind. But occasionally I would wake in the middle of the night and cry. These sobbings were becoming less and less frequent and I had begun to take comfort from the fact that I knew wherever Bill was, he would want me to be happy and continue living.

'Is anything wrong? Did I say something to upset you?' The stranger was looking at me with concern.

'No, no! There's nothing wrong. I'm sorry. A sad memory just passed through my mind.' I said.

I stole a few glances at my host. He looked at me with concern and I noticed a sad look in those otherwise warm, glittering brown eyes.

African Widow

by Sydia Gweshe

How sweet were the days
When he was still living—
My husband.
Oh, I wonder, in my hut,
What life I shall now lead.

Harsh and vindictive
Were his brothers.
How sad I felt
As they took our belongings.

The eldest proposed love.
His words were like venom to me.
He seized all our property.

Now my children suffer
Because of their cruel uncle

An heir not justified.

When I was a child

by Shingirai Pensado

When I was a child
Of course I knew there was mother and father
But my mother
Divorced my father
And tells me to be good and moral.

When I was a child
I grew up respecting my elders
But the one who is my stepfather
Married four times and had many children
He asks me to be a good mother.

When I was a child
My father divorced my mother
And married another woman.
My father has numerous children
He tells me to behave myself.

When I was a child
I was told my father's wife had married three times.
She has many children with different fathers.
She is a hard woman
And advises me to be gentle.

I am puzzled at their preaching
I am afraid to follow in their footsteps!

Hapana Basa

Hapana Basa—No Work

by Memory Dete

Everywhere he went, Fungai met bold signs which said very clearly, 'Hapana Basa—No Work'. He had spent six solid months hunting for a job. A month ago he had been lucky enough to get interviews at two companies. Both had gone very well and he had been optimistic. He could hardly wait for the post to hear the outcome, but his heart sank on a Monday evening when he'd come home to find two 'regret letters' awaiting him.

Fungai was very depressed and for some days he considered giving up job-hunting. He changed his mind, however, when he remembered that his welfare, as well as that of his aged parents, depended on him alone. He knew that he could not give up. He was desperate for a job.

Fungai's parents had sold much of their livestock and grain to earn enough to provide for his training. They were now looking to him to get a job and begin a new life of his own. Their money would go to waste if finding a job proved to be impossible and their despair would be great. His mother had hinted to him that she expected a *muroora* in the near future as she was finding it difficult to manage hard work.

'I am no longer as young and active as I used to be,' she told him. 'Soon I shall need a helping hand. My eyes are beginning to fail me. I cannot see what lies ahead of me, be it near or far, when the sun shines brightly.'

His father had added: 'We are losing our strength and soon we will be completely helpless like little babies. But what makes us happy is that you have completed your training and it will not be long before you find a job. Your mother and I have no qualms about the future because we know that when the time comes you will look after us, as we took care of you.' These words rang in Fungai's mind and it was this that gave him the determination to go on and on job-hunting.

He rented a small, single room which he thought was like a prison cell. The dirty walls were a dull greyish-brownish-white. The room was bare except for a wooden bench, a primus stove, a few blankets and a small suitcase in which Fungai kept his clothing. At night he slept on the cold, hard floor and in the ceiling big rats made squeaking noises which disturbed his sleep. This was the only lodging which Fungai could afford but he knew that with the acquisition of a job, things would improve for him.

When he set out next for his job hunt, the first thing his eyes rested on was an overturned bin. Bits of rubbish were scattered around the area and he noticed that more rubbish was flying around than was in the bin. A black dog, with its bones clearly visible through its matted skin, was inside the bin searching frantically for food. Eventually the animal emerged slowly with its tail lowered, looking very mournful. It was obviously hungry but had not found food. Fungai placed himself in the same position as the famished dog.

As he hurried along the street, he saw a group of young men who were sitting on the grass with their feet in the drain. Two were smoking and the other three had bottles of beer close at hand. Fungai knew that if he stopped to talk with them they would relate the same old story: they had quit looking for jobs and were finding solace in smoking and drinking. As he walked passed them, they turned to look at him enviously. He looked very much as if he was on his way to work, dressed in his smart clothes.

'We're in the same boat,' he wanted to stop and tell them. 'Except that I must never give up as you have done.'

He visited two garages in the industrial sites but they were in no need of a mechanic. With his spirits beginning to flag he went to a third garage which he could see from across the road.

In the neat reception area he felt the coolness of the room from the two big fans whirring on the ceiling. There were two other rooms which were marked as those of the Managing Director and Accountant.

Fungai had glanced into the workshop before entering the reception and the smell of oil made him wish he was part of the activity, working on the numerous cars that were parked and jacked up. The mechanics, who were dressed in greasy overalls, walked in and out of the workshop holding in their arms their tools and implements.

Funagi felt apprehensive as he waited for the secretary to finish speaking on the phone. When she put down the receiver, he told her he was seeking employment and had brought all his credentials. The secretary, frowning, examined him from head to toe. Fungai disliked her cold stares. He glanced down at her hands and noticed her long, red nails and thought they looked like claws. He imagined them digging deep into his neck and he shuddered at the thought. The secretary's tone was cold and dismissive.

'I don't care about your qualifications. Anyway, we're in no need of a mechanic. And a word of advice before you go: apply in writing if you're seeking employment!'

It took all of Fungai's self-control not to give the proud young secretary a piece of his mind and his hand burned to slap her across her powdered cheeks. But she didn't seem aware of her rudeness and turned back to her typewriter. The sound of the keys played on his nerves making him more angry and frustrated. He stood up to go but just then the Managing Director's door was flung open:

'Molly!' the man who emerged, shouted to the secretary.

'Sir?'

Fungai noticed that Molly had lost her authoritativeness and had now become very alert and looked a bit afraid. He, too, felt a certain fear sweep over him for the man, who was taking long strides into the office, had an angry, no-nonsense expression on his face. He was a tall, thin man with a curling moustache. He wore glasses and had a bald patch in the middle of his head.

He was furious about something and had grown quite red. His one hand was clenched tightly into a fist and the other was continually running through what remained of his hair.

Fungai wondered whether he should just disappear quietly out of the office.

'I just had a call from the Workshop Manager,' Molly's boss spoke in a booming, angry voice, which Fungai was sure could be heard for miles around. It seemed odd that the man should have such a loud voice and it contrasted with his otherwise lean features.

'He says he's quit his job because he's been employed by another garage for higher wages.'

'That was a very thoughtless act,' said Molly calmly. 'He should have informed you of his plans to leave beforehand.'

'He's put me into a tight fix,' her boss said, taking out a packet of cigarettes and a lighter from his pocket. 'I can't do without a Workshop Manager. Its impossible to do the double job of supervision and the work in my office.'

After several puffs at his cigarette, he appeared a bit calmer. Then his eye fell on Fungai, who had sat down on an armchair close to the door.

'Who are you?' he demanded rudely.

'Fungai Gwati.'

'What do you want?'

Molly put forth an explanation: 'I thought he'd left. He's looking for a job.'

The boss studied Fungai closely and looked thoughtful. 'Ever worked before?'

'I completed my training six months ago.'

'I didn't ask when you completed your training but whether you'd worked before,' he shouted. 'Do you understand English?'

'I do, Sir,'

'Then answer my question correctly.'

'I haven't worked before.'

The boss turned back to Molly. 'I'll have to replace that smart aleck with one of the more experienced guys in the workshop. That means I'll need another mechanic.'

He turned back to Fungai: 'Since you popped in at the right moment, I'll give you a try. I'm not promising anything. Come and see me on Monday and then I'll have come to a decision whether to take you on or not.'

Fungai's spirits were starting to rise. There was no mistaking the Managing Director was a hard man who would expect perfection at all times. He knew that he would always live in fear of him.

He left the office after giving Molly a victorious look although he would only know on Monday whether he was victorious or not.

He was deep in thought as he walked to the bus terminus. He remembered that other occasion when he had had two interviews in one week and nothing had come of them. It could happen again, so he did not want to be too optimistic.

'Only time will determine my happiness or despair,' he thought as he joined the bus queue.

These Days

by Ama Ata Aidoo

Last night
I could not help but recall
how Mother ended
those precious lessons in
personal grooming:

'. . . and remember
to keep a cheerful face:
it costs nothing, and
will do you no end of good.'

Last night,
staring in the face of
that
special
plague
which—the ancients must have foretold—
shall come to
end all human hopes,

You and I
discovered
—if we hadn't before—

And we moaned about a ruined world
doubly ruined
for our children
    by
epidemics of rolling tanks,
scuds,
other missile sorties and
the glee of
foolish old men
cheering at skies
exploding into
flowery flames
            to
rain
death
    destruction
            despair.

so
it was not easy.
But we tried, very hard,
to go shopping for
laughter.

As another lightning ripped
    through the darkening air.

Who Lives Next Door

by Lilian Masitera

My tap-tapping on the typewriter
Invites an intruder—
Little Winfrieda

At the tender age of three
She flees from her parents
To fiddle freely around my flat

When her mother comes over
Checking
Whether her daughter is a bother
We gather at the typewriter
Laughing
Three women in unison.

If her father comes over
Checking
Whether his daughter is a bother
I shrink
Because while he gathers his daughter
He winks lustfully at me.

My bang-banging on saucepans
While making supper
Is a nightmare
It invites my other neighbours

Their starving son stands at my window
Sniffing the tantalising odour
Wafting from my cooking.

His mother raps at the door:
'Do you have money that I can borrow?
My husband gets paid tomorrow!'
Her stories are stale
Her begging endless
But how else can she survive
With five mouths to feed?

My counting of coins
Is halted
By the ringing of the phone
'Hello?'

I hear raucous music
I hear clatters of laughter
I hear glasses clinking
I hear coins rattling
I hear holed-up hell
Then I hear his rasping voice

'Hello?'

That, there is my neighbour
Dating me
By phone
From a pub

He acts big shot about town
While his wife seeks alms
In my house.

Behind the Curtain

by Tawona Mtshiya

Gradually the applause sounded
louder, louder to a deafening melody
The neon lights flashed faster, blending
GREEN, RED, BLACK, into a blinding, suspicious
mind-blowing sight.

I looked around into the invisible audience
SUDDENLY! my mind was torn
between the floating stage curtains
and a shadow splashed by
the VICIOUS blends of the lights.

For a moment I froze in fear,
Fear which I had paid a price for.
I touched my seat around . . . only
to touch my shadow;
the audience continued
applauding.

How I wish I could jump from my seat
and run to seek refuge . . . But . . .
I had paid a price.

Like a circus band drumming for a
nervous trapeze team . . . the
invisible audience joined me in
watching the curtains slowly split open.

What a sight resting behind those curtains!
A sight I had longed for, but
a sight my imagination would not share with
my being.

'Jump onto the stage! You are the
ACTRESS
ACTRESS
ACTRESS!
My mother's voice echoed painfully
into my ears amid the deafening applause
of the invisible audience
'But mom, the chains . . . the chains
of bondage.'

'My child, drag them along
for . . . behind those curtains lies
FREEDOM, HOPE and TRIUMPH.'

The River God's Hunger

by Sonia Gomez

I
At dawn in the Namib,
ebony striations of beetles
ascend rippling gold dunes.
At the wind-cut crests
they stand on their heads,
Atlantic fog breaking on their bodies,
condensation, silver droplets
glittering down until
they have drunk their fill of ocean,
enough for the scorching day ahead,
and at the first slant of light
they scatter and vanish
into shifting topaz sands.

II
The train swaggers
into Hwange at midnight,
hot stars giving way to electric lights
fluttering with moths.
We're in second class
looking down the line to economy,
where coal workers
off for the weekend,
strut down the platform
in a boistrous, drunken jostle,
loading up two-kilogram rations
of fine, white maize meal,
or a mangy chicken
held snug in an armpit.

Boys come slipping from shadows,
crowned with enamel bowls
of oranges and
brown-speckled boiled eggs.
We buy some shrivelled fruit
and watch the woman
with an ebony carved face,
ugly enough to tempt the river god
to send rain.
Train whistles and pulls away
toward the dry Zambezi,
and the ebony woman
standing on the platform
escapes into fluttering darkness.
Inside, the men grow silent,
going home to parching land,
they lean their dark gleaming faces
against old teak, and the purple night
drifts in through open sash windows.

III
The sky turns to copper.
I can feel the air electric with thunder
and the smell of earth.
I wait for the first drops,
eyes closed, palms open,
waiting for rivers to run,
I breathe slowly
lightning breaks
over the jacaranda tree,
a purple flash of shadow,
and then, dark, silver sheets of rain,
a quenching unmerciful torrent.
Dust turns instantly to cool mud,
and by noon thousands of winged
termites lift out of red earth,
like silver veined spirits released.

Although I Need Some Help

by Dudzai Medi

Although I need some help
There—and there!
Not here and there!
The world doesn't see what I do for myself.

I cook sadza for family and visitors.
I do the washing of clothes and blankets.
I collect water myself and bath.
I make my bed and sleep on it.
No-one accompanies me to the toilet.
So, where is your help?

If you see me begging,
Teach me to work for food.
If you see me hungry,
Show me the river to feed myself.

Don't judge me by my appearance,
A wheelchair and a pair of crutches
Are means of transport.
They are not part of my body.
I've got legs—with blood and veins!

Why should you gossip about me?
You are my closest relatives.
If I were fit and strong,
I would have fought
Till you accepted me—
As a human being like you.

Claim Our Rights

by Bianca Mahlunge

Give us our rights
We are the mothers
of tomorrow's leaders—
Not baby-producing machines.
Give us our rights!

We are up long before dawn
Toiling in the fields
But benefit nothing—
Just feeding our babies

Women, let's stand up
And show them
We can build a nation!
Let's show them
We can claim our future!

Let's demonstrate now
That we women
Will claim our rights!

Don't Blame the Creator

by Maureen Mataranyika

In the beginning all was well.
The earth rotated on its axis—
Round and round it went
Until handed over to mankind
Virgin land, rich and green—
Valleys, filled with flowers in bloom.

The seas lay in glamorous beauty
And pure oceans rolled by night and day.
Trees swayed gently in the breeze
As clean dusk fell to end every perfect day.

Then came clearing of the land for cocaine plantations.
Industrial waste destroyed nature's attractions.
Atomic bombs and other deadly weapons
Took their toll—in manmade desert formations
And filth.

After all, we can't blame the creator.

Looking Over My Left Shoulder

by Cornelia Bullen-Smith

'Watch out,' he said, 'the fleas are jumping off.' We were both crouching next to the dead cat with the broken neck. I stepped back hastily. He was right. One of the fleas had hopped onto the sleeve of my shirt. I squashed it before it had time to crawl closer.

'I'll fetch some newspaper,' I mumbled and walked blindly into the house. One of the children was curled up in the armchair, reading, the other was looking for the cat.

'Micky, Micky, Micky,' he called.

We covered the body with newspaper and then picked it up. It felt stiff and hard like frozen fish. 'It has been raining cats,' I thought, losing control over the pictures in my head. It must have been dead for quite a while. The dogs most probably killed it just after we left for the Saturday afternoon visit to Granny. Granny loves cats. She has four—big, fat ones.

The white kitten with the grey ears stumbled into our family after a vicious thunderstorm had blown through the Westdene area of Benoni. We had arrived there some days before from Harare. We were in transit, on the way to Cape Town. The serpentine channels of bureaucracy had caught up with us in Zimbabwe and had hissed a thirty day notice at us. We were forced to leave the country where we had been welcome for some years. Inadequate information and senseless shortsightedness from officials meant that our residence permit was not renewed.

We tumbled and struggled through thirty days of frantic organising. The children were excited by the prospect of moving back into our house, close to cousins and long-missed friends, back to the sea and the mountains—back to what we used to call home.

I was tight-lipped and tense, forcing myself to look only one day ahead. The furrow between my eyebrows seemed to be deeper each morning that I took the time to look at myself.

Only weeks before I had assembled many lists of 'why we should stay' and 'why we should go back' in an attempt to find the right solution for us. Did Nelson Mandela's release mean we should end our self-imposed exile, or should we wait until the Group Areas Act had been abolished as we had initially said we would?

When the Zimbabwe Government took the decision off our hands and told us to leave, I suddenly knew I didn't want to go just then. I cried on Tafadzwa's shoulder. Even if she would come to visit us as she promised over and over again, I felt already how different this friendship would be. I knew we would not be able to stand somewhere in Cape Town, holding hands while talking to each other, without feeling watched and self-conscious.

I also felt so tired—not like a fighter any more.

The kitten was wet and miserable, hardly a week old. It survived our clumsy attempts to keep it alive long enough for us to realise that it didn't know how to lap. We fed it with a syringe and even before it became strong enough to hold its head up again and stand on its own, we decided, against all reason, to adopt it.

The house in Cape Town was empty when we arrived. We entered through an open side door. How often had I tried to imagine this situation. How often I had dreamt about feeling the tiles under my bare feet again, running my hands over the wooden top of the kitchen counter, entering the room where the child was born.

What a fool I had been to think that after five years the house would still be filled with laughter, with our joy at being a family full of plans and idealism. The building was cold and mucky, the garden seemed idiotic with plastic pots and cigarette butts. The christmas tree was burnt.

The sun helped and so did friends. They covered us with warm attention and allowed us to knot onto the strings of togetherness that we had cut off when we fled. They invited us to their homes for meals, let us talk about Zimbabwe and listened without ever saying 'why did you leave us?'

We started breathing deeply again. Yes, we had finally come to the end of a long journey. The trauma of the move was over. The dogs arrived by plane, the furniture in a truck. As we started to unpack the boxes with our belongings, finding places for toys, clothes and books, I slowly began to accept that this would be home again. In time we would paint, fill the cracks in the walls, plant the hedge again and make things grow. I was ready to settle down. It would be a good place again.

The kitten learned how to lap and began eating meat. It grew and became stronger. It had a big, knobbly belly button and lots of fleas. We called it 'Mikyas'.

We found a job, selected a school for the children, organised a cheque account. The telephone was connected, the first letters arrived in the postbox. Instead of waking up with a mouth full of sorrow and regret for lost friends and bitter feelings about cut-off opportunities, I began to smile again.

I became experienced in walking through a huge supermarket, ignoring all the ridiculous items made of attractively coloured plastic, packaged in shiny cling wrap. What we needed were basic foodstuffs, like milk and butter, bread and cheese. And tins of catfood, of course— 'Pamper—for the cat in your life'.

I learned to live with white faces around me. I lost track of the time since we arrived and I stopped telling stories about our life in Zimbabwe. I began calculating in Rand.

We fell into a routine and I made decisions again. I didn't want all these plastic bags and I didn't like the pressure the children had to cope with at school. I refused the plastic bags and spoke to the teachers.

As I walked along the beach, feeling the cool sand between my toes, making plans for the weeks to come, I knew I still had a chance. I was alive again.

The moon was full on Saturday. Rainclouds gathered below the mountain as we drove home. The body of the cat lay in front of the sidedoor. It was still wet with the saliva from the biting dogs. The eyes were open, the head twisted awkwardly.

We made a fire that night and we cried. A thunderstorm found us huddled together, a family full of sorrow, plans and idealism.

The next day we planted four sunflowers in our garden.

Zimbabwe Women Writers (particularly in the rural areas) need manual and electric typewriters.

Please support women writing in the countryside

No Application Form

by Nomathemba Mkandla

There is no application form
To be disabled.
If there were
I do not imagine myself filling one in.

It is difficult to live in this world.
Some people look at me
As a useless creature,
Yet they do not know—

They do not know
That they are lost
That I do things they can't.

In the streets,
Their attention is drawn.
They stare
As if I've come from Heaven.
Some look with merciful faces,
Some with eyes of ignorance.

So if you see a disabled person
Do not laugh.
It may happen to you
Because there is no application form.

If there were,
I do not imagine myself filling one in.

The Dam

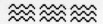

by Pat Chiyangwa

Still blue waters—
I watch and daydream
As fish swim.
And birds fly to and fro
Welcoming the cool breeze.
I bubble with pride

This is the dam.
Long before its existence
On that land
Stood my little hut
And others too.

I got my water from the spring
For my cattle
My dogs
And for my little garden too.

This is the dam
That helped me

Far away from it now
Stands my house—
My orchard
My livestock
Now far away from it
I turn the tap
And water runs.

This is the dam.

Rain

by Ruth Weiss

Firo awoke. Her left arm felt stiff and numb. She touched it, felt the damp, and rubbed it against the thin blanket. Water was dripping through the thatch. She had heard her mother say only last night that she would have to repair it, had hoped it wouldn't rain.

It was raining now. Firo lay still for a moment, listening to the howling of the wind, she noticed that her little brother stirred. She got up carefully so as not to disturb him. Firo had no watch, but she knew it was time to get up. She always woke before five, just as she always fell asleep the instant her head was down, after she had helped her mother with the cooking and washing up. Usually she rose with the sun. But Firo knew that today it would not be light for a while. Not until the storm had cleared.

She tiptoed to the bucket she had filled with water the night before, scooped a little into the basin next to it to wash her face and hands, pulled the blue dress, her school uniform, over her head, smoothed her hair with her mother's comb. She picked up her sandals and pushed them into the plastic bag she used as a schoolbag; no point in putting them on, it would be too wet. A flash of lightning illuminated the hut, showing her the sleeping form of her brother and the two maize cobs she had smeared with peanut butter. She threw them into the bag, sipped at a

173

little of the water in the bucket and straightened up. She was ready for the day.

As she opened the door, carefully, so as not to wake anyone, she shivered in fear as another flash of lightning streaked across the dark clouds, instantly followed by the enormous sound of thunder. Her mother would not get up now. She would not be able to go to the fields. She would wait until the storm had blown itself out. Firo cheered up a little. The storm would also keep the monkeys away. If so, perhaps there was no need to go to the fields in the afternoon when she came back from school. Usually that was one of her jobs, chasing the monkeys, cheeky creatures, digging up seeds and stealing the crops. She glanced at the small pile of stones she had heaped up near the granary as ammunition against the monkeys.

Firo was fourteen, the oldest of six children and the only one who went to school, the only one in the village. The others were babies or toddlers. Firo was proud of her status. She could speak English, just like the men, not only Shona like the women and children.

All the same, today it would have been nice to stay at home. She bent her head, passed the hut where her mother slept with her younger brothers and sisters, past the larger hut of her father's second wife who had lived with them with her first-born for a year now. Firo knew the way. She had walked it countless times, which was just as well, for she would have strayed now, in this terrifying darkness, with the noise of the storm all around her, the hard earth turned to slippery mud. A gust of wind almost made her lose her balance. The rain battered her face, water seeped into her nostrils, made her gasp for breath. Usually it took her three hours to get to school, twelve miles away. Today she would be late, if she made it at all. Slowly she walked on, feeling her way.

'*Mangwanani.*' She heard the greeting, curtseyed and returned it in the correct manner. She knew where she was—in the next village, close to the kraal of Kefasi Marimbo, a member of the village committee. She often passed his wife on her way to the fields.

Firo stood still and leaned against the fence for a moment. The fury of the wind had abated but it was still raining. Time to move on. She heard the man calling, asking if she wanted to come into the kitchen, he had tea ready. She hesitated, then meekly followed the invitation. It was warm inside. He had a fire going. Gratefully she accepted the mug of boiling hot liquid.

Kefasi spoke softly, 'My wife is ill. I will see her now.'

How good he was, Firo decided, making tea for a sick wife. Would her father...? She dismissed the thought. There was no need. There was herself to do such things and now the second wife. Marimbo was old. He had no sons and his daughters had left home.

'You should dry your dress.' He stood close to the door, holding the big mug of tea for his sick wife. Firo inclined her head shyly and he nodded and shut the door behind him. Swiftly the young girl slipped out of the blue dress, spreading it out in front of the three stones inbetween which the flames licked lazily. She knelt in front of the fire, looked around for another piece of wood, felt comfortable for the first time that morning. She thought of the English lesson, recalled the poem she had learnt.

'Oh, mother, look at the brightness of this day,
this special, bridal day
when sun and moon,
day and night,
embrace each other in blissful joy.'

Perhaps one day, she too, would write such words? Lost in her own thoughts, Firo had not heard the man return. Embarrassed, she covered her small breasts with her hands, reached out for the dress, already half-dry on the hard dung floor. She was conscious of his closeness, heard his loud breathing.

'Sekuru!' she stammered. He reached out, held her arm, her thin body. She pushed at him, helpless in his grip. She knew she had to fight, but felt she was not fighting

175

hard enough. She was thrown down, her clawed hands held, the arched back pressed down, the thin legs spread apart.

Two hours later she was at school. The man had a donkey cart and he took her close to the building. She walked the last few steps alone. No one saw them. No one cared. The rain had turned to a drizzle. Everyone was late. Firo was not the last to arrive. Lessons began.

'Oh mother, look at the brightness of the day . . .'
No one noticed that Firo was crying.

During the next few months, Firo continued to go to school. She was no longer the proud, happy girl everyone once noticed. She cringed when spoken to, was no longer the first to answer questions in class. She stayed as long as she could in the fields. And each day she bypassed Marimbo's kraal. Nor did the man visit her father's village.

Five months later she could no longer hide her condition. She confessed to her mother what had happened on that day of the storm. That night all her fears came true: her father beat her: he picked up an axe and beat her with the handle. He was so enraged that he did not seem to see or care where he struck: on the girl's face, her arms, legs, back, even her swollen belly. She no longer knew whether the screams she heard were her own or those of the children. The pain was everywhere. Nothing seemed to matter. She heard the crack when her left arm broke and barely realised that her mother had thrown herself between them. Instantly her father turned on his wife, shouting, as he applied the pick handle to her unresisting body.

'You . . . you spoilt your daughter . . . who will pay *lobola* for her now! Where did she learn these tricks, eh? You whore, do you go with strange men when I'm in the store?'

Firo's father had opened a small store in the new growth point, but he had never taken Firo's mother there, only the second wife, who stood behind the counter and was often given special gifts, like the cloth from which she had made herself a new dress only the day before.

176

Firo crept to the door and into the yard, made it to the path which led to the field, found a soft heap of sand close to the antheap and fainted.

When she came to her senses, it was early morning. She could see soft light against the clouds. She sat up and saw her arm dangle useless at her side. She noticed a bundle of clothing close to her. Crawling on her side, she came closer and saw to her dismay that it was her mother, unconscious, blood seeping from her mouth, nose and ears.

Wildly, Firo looked around, but there was no one in sight. There would be no help from her father's home. She stumbled towards the tarred road and was fortunate that a truck driver driving his early morning load, was shocked by her appearance. He carried the injured woman to his vehicle and drove them to the nearest hospital.

Both were admitted. No one asked any questions, it was so obvious what had happened. A pregnant girl, a wife who had been beaten.

On the sixth day, Firo was discharged, her arm still in plaster, but well enough to look after the children of one of the nurses. A policeman appeared at her mother's bedside, asked if she had any charge to make. The matron had notified the police of the woman's serious internal injuries. She shook her head. What was the point. Even if the village court found her husband guilty, he would not take her back. She would have to go to town, try and survive with Firo and the baby. It would be best if it was a boy.

This was also what the man said, when eventually Firo went to him. Kefasi Marimbo found Firo early one morning, cowering on the same spot where he had seen her that morning of the storm, six months before. He greeted her without enthusiasm. He knew, of course, what had happened and was aware that her father had kicked out her mother as well as Firo.

Marimbo looked down at the weeping girl. Finally he nodded. 'Very well. You can stay. And—I won't pay *roora*. You're no longer pure. I hope it will be a boy.'

Firo knelt and touched his hand, not looking up, murmuring her gratitude. He nodded again. 'Hm. Perhaps you father will take your mother back. I'll see. I mean, she didn't charge him.' Then he added. 'Yes, I hope it is a son. I need a strong daughter-in-law.'

A son, yes. I hope so too. And if it is a girl, I will never send her to school, or, if I do, she'll never, ever walk in the rain, thought Firo.

Amai

by Rosemary Smith-Kebe
(On the death of Amai Sally Mugabe)

We call you Mother
With respect and love.
First Lady
First Mother:
Amai

Example to the Nation
Mother to us all,
We shall miss you.
We bless you,
Amai.

Mother to the Nation,
Example to us all,
First Lady,
First Mother:
Goodbye.

You Lived

(Dedicated to Uncle Robert Chimanda)

by Faith Fungayi Chimanda

The days you lived
You brightened my life,
You made me happy,
Memories live in me now

I know you will be happy
Beyond this ordinary world.
We will come too—
I will come too.

The order of life
Disturbs many—
Myself included—
But now I know you are no more.

AIDS

by Rudo Mufute

Here I am—
The unpredicted—
The most outrageous—
A rabid, ravenous wolf

I destroy your immune system.
I disrupt your body.
Nothing can be done.
You are exposed
To fatality.

Once I invade,
I am the victor.
My victims are nurtured
Well into the grave.

My World

by Anita van der Heiden

The world to me is dark,
It hasn't always been this way.
The year it happened well I mark
But that I'd rather not say.

My life now depends on sound
Which comes from far and near.
I know what's happening around,
And therefore do not fear.

The sounds of cars going by,
The sounds I hear above.
I long to see the bright blue sky
And all God's creation I love.

I had my sight till I was nine
Nine happy years and gay.
Those nine years of bright sunshine,
Now night and day I pray.

I pray my sight may still return
My speech and movements as well,
For these my heart does yearn,
But only God can tell.

The Photograph

by Monica Skeete

A faint shirring in the distance and then the sound became gradually more insistent until it was an urgent demanding clamour which abruptly jerked Mary to full consciousness. Her hand shot out automatically and firmly pressed the knob that put a stop to the unwelcome intrusion. She always felt a little ungrateful for giving the faithful old clock such short shrift. It had been a birthday present from her mother.

Talking about birthdays, today was her thirtieth. Thirty? And how, for God's sake, had she got there? She felt no different from other days but no doubt some of her friends thought that she was settling on the shelf. She decided that she should ignore the stupid jibes.

She turned over and, as always, her eyes met those of her father staring a little sadly from the framed photograph on the wall. What would he have thought of her if he could see her now?

The morning traffic clonked and bustled as usual on the road outside and then subsided, leaving just a few late stragglers trailing in its wake as she put the rubbish in the bin beside her little gate and collected the mail from its recess in the wall.

One envelope with strange bright-coloured stamps stood out clearly among the drab brown collection of bills. Mary turned it over curiously. It was an airmail letter and not one of those pestering advertising leaflets that had suddenly started circulating around the island. She went back into the bedroom and sat in her usual chair just under the photograph. She turned the envelope back and forth and then slowly slit it open.

Feverishly she unfolded the single sheet of sharply typed script. She felt the same sense of excitement as when she used to watch her mother opening letters from her brothers, Charles and Rupert, while they were migrant workers abroad.

Charles had been working on a sugarcane plantation in Florida and Rupert was in the oilfields in Dutch Aruba in the south Caribbean. They used to send money regularly and Mary always accompanied her mother to the post office to cash the postal orders.

'Your brothers don't forget us,' Ma would say. 'God keep them. They will come back one day.'

These remittances meant new clothes and goodies in the larder. Ma insisted on buying a picnic ham every month and she made a great occasion of cooking it and spotting it all over with cloves. She cut thick slices and loaded them on to the plates.

'Eat, child!' she'd say. 'You're lucky. I never had these things when I was young.'

Mary barely nibbled a tiny bit as she watched the white fat momentarily masking Ma's lips on its swift passage into her avid mouth. After a time she grew to hate the sight of ham.

Charles had remained in the United States and married a white American girl. At first there were frequent letters and photographs of their first plump infant with brown curls and delightful round eyes.

'He looks just like me,' Ma said, 'and he has a good colour too. Could almost pass for white,' she giggled, holding the photograph at arm's length to see it better.

Mary thought the baby looked like the faded photograph of her father which hung on the wall of her mother's bedroom. She often sat under it when her mother was out and stared at the face of this man with a firm thin line for a mouth which yet had the faint suggestion of a smile at the corners. She could barely remember him. He must have been tall because she did remember how far away the floor seemed when he held her up on his shoulders.

Ma never spoke of him now. Whenever Mary mentioned him and tried to ask a few questions, it was just as if a door was banged in her face. 'He left us. He never looked back. Show me anything you have that he ever gave you.'

Mary always felt that there must be some way she could defend him but the overwhelming evidence of his guilt always seemed to flow over them and drown her into silence.

Rupert came home once and brought some pretty dresses for Mary and her mother.

'Look at my boy! What a man he is now!' Ma gushed at the neighbours drawing the attention of all who would listen. For two delirious weeks they were happy together. Mary adored this big brother who petted and treasured her and she experienced the thrill of being part of a family, but he soon went on to New York because, as he said, there was nothing for him on a small island. After a while his letters became fewer and fewer and then they stopped altogether.

Ma worked hard to keep Mary in secondary school.

'I had to leave school when I was twelve but that must not happen to you,' she'd say.

'Did you like school, Ma?' The question had never occurred to her before. Ma had always been there just to be the provider and consoler.

'I wanted to learn so much but I could not go regularly because I had to stay home and look after my two little brothers.'

Mary knew only vaguely about these uncles whom she had never seen but she felt a momentary sense of reproach for these parasites who had taken so much from her mother and gone without a backward glance. So many of the island's menfolk had disappeared for ever—part of the surplus population bred for export. She wanted to reach out and sympathise but she said nothing and the moment passed.

Ma nagged if Mary did not seem to be applying herself to her school work. Once she was about to retort angrily, but Ma unexpectedly threw her arms around her murmuring tearfully, 'Only the best, the best for you.'

Mary was not outstanding but she passed her exams and tried to be a credit to her mother. All her friends were eager to get out and go to the big exciting countries—the United States of America especially. But Mary loved the beach and the sound of the waves swishing on the rocks, just a stone's throw from their home. She felt secure in the warmth of her familiar world. Once when she was dressing to go to the farewell party of one of her friends, she caught Ma's eyes regarding her with a kind of wistful resignation.

'I suppose you'll be going next,' she said in a whisper.

'No, Ma! No!' Mary was surprised at the fierceness of her own conviction. She finally did a secretarial course and secured a potentially lucrative job with a real estate agent.

She enjoyed the attention of several young men who came and went but avoided getting into serious amorous entanglements because the spectre of desertion had to be checked at all costs. She could not say that life was dull but whenever she could, she still sneaked into her mother's room and sat before the photograph of her father. She often wondered why it had not been removed since Ma hardly ever looked at it without a contemptuous snort.

Then, one day, Mary came in barefoot from the back yard and found Ma staring dejectedly at the photograph while two big tears rolled down her cheeks. Mary had backed away sensing instinctively that she should not intrude in the private agony of her parents' past. She still wished that she could tell her father that she had not forgotten him: that she was not sitting in judgment on him even if she never really understood why he had never communicated with them.

Ma had always been a hard worker and never had a day's illness. Then, without any warning, it happened. She was drinking a glass of lemonade and it started running down the sides of her mouth.

'Ma! What you doing?' Mary said jokingly from her end of the little table where they always ate together. Instead of answering, Ma flopped forward and that was all. She had had a stroke. After a period in hospital, she remained paralysed on one side and never spoke again.

Mary cared for her, remaining in her room as often as she could. Ma, who had been so vocal, was now left to balance in silence the gains and losses of her life.

Mary noticed that she would stare almost fixedly at the photograph for a long time. She thought it must distress her and one day decided to take it down. She was startled by the grunting agitation that came from the bed. Mary looked back, half in alarm, half in surprise. Ma's face was distorted with pain.

'You don't want me to move it'

Gently she hung it back on the rusty nail. Ma calmed down and continued to watch it day by day.

As suddenly as she had been stricken, she just passed away one morning just after Mary had left for work, believing that everything was as usual.

Mary continued to live in the little house with the ghosts of her family. She redecorated Ma's bedroom and moved into it but left her father's photograph where it had always been.

And now, today, she was holding this letter from a solicitor in faraway Honduras. He had been instructed by her father's will to sell his property and send the proceeds to his last child and only daughter, if she was still alive— $500,000.00

Woman for Sale

by Egely Donadi

Why trade your womanhood for a dollar
Daughter of the soil?
Why sell yourself for a piece of bread
My sister?

Like the common path to the river
Day and night you are trodden upon
Like a mat at their doorstep
You suck up their dirt.

You destroy your life
To quench their unquenchable desires
Then old and overused—like a rag—
You are thrown on the rubbish pit

You are toilet paper
Not good for the eyes
There you lie
So soon forgotten
Flushed away.

The Setting Sun

by Mable Chiquye

The woman was in great pain
Her eyes were glassy
Her face contorted
Her words were forced and slurred.

One glance at her ashen face
And frail body
Revealed the truth.
One, two, three, I could count the ribs.

Bedridden for a year and a half
Her tight thin-lipped mouth revealed
The suffering she had endured
Tears of pity poured from my eyes.

Oh God! How can this be?
What kind of suffering is this?
This is more than a person can endure.
I wiped her forehead and said a silent prayer.

'Please, will you get me some water?'
The agony in her voice was excruciating
I looked at her
I seemed to be in a dream.

Instead of giving water, I turned away
A strong urge drove me away.
Blindly I walked as if in a trance
Then slammed into something hard.

I looked up to see what it was
Instead of the door it was a wall.
My senses became normal again
I returned to the woman and gave her water.

Her hand was so frail that it shook
Tears of gratitude welled in her eyes
My heart bled with remorse
Oh God! Save humankind!

Do you think I mean the setting of the sun?
No, it is the destruction of humankind
By this cruel immune-to-medicine disease
Called AIDS

Do you think the woman survived?
No, a few days later she died
Just as thousands are dying now.
How can we assuage this suffering?

I Came to Town

by Margret Nzuwa

High buildings:
Buildings in town,
Reach up so high
I sometimes think
They touch the sky.

They are higher
Than the highest trees
And I think they are going
To follow me.

A hundred windows
Perhaps there are more
A hundred windows
And just one door.

There isn't a step
And there isn't a stair
How do people get up there?

<u>Drought</u>

by Rachael Chitongo

It is hot like hell.
Tell me what to do.
No water, no food.
All over, it is dry.

All the rivers are dry.
All the dams are dry.
All the lakes are dry.
Are the oceans dry too?

No grass for the animals.
No water for the birds.
No leaves for the giraffes.
No marulas for the elephants.

No water, no Life.
Dead buffaloes, birds, dogs,
Rhinos, foxes, pangolins.
Please God, do something!

People are suffering
Day and night.
Hard conditions.
How can we survive without water?

God, save us
From this drought!

My First Problem as a Woman

by Christine Muranda

I could tell by the mask he wore as he sat at the dinner table that all was not well.

'I've had enough,' he said in a sort of whisper. He had barely touched his food. I quickly removed the dishes and the uneaten meal from the table and walked out of the room with my head spinning. I wanted to scream but no voice came out.

His strange behaviour had gone on for quite some time. He came home very late most nights and his drinking habits were so bad that at times he had problems getting up in the mornings.

On several occasions he had given lame excuses to his boss for not going to work. He would spend the day in bed, wake up late in the afternoon and bath. Then he'd be off, coming home in the early hours of the morning.

On this day he was not drunk, nor was he late, but I could see that all was not well. Why is he behaving like this? I asked myself. We have been paid our wages. We don't have much cash but we have managed to pay our accounts, the maid, and buy food. Why, oh why is this happening?

Tears started rolling down my cheeks. I went into the bedroom and saw that our two-month-old boy was fast asleep. I went into the bathroom and splashed water on my face and returned some minutes later a bit refreshed. Then I went to bed.

I don't know how many hours passed before I fell asleep but when I awoke I saw him sleeping beside me fully clothed except for his shoes and cap. I switched on the light and looked at the clock. It was 4am. I was sleepy and fell asleep again.

A loud knock woke us. We had slept late since it was Saturday and he was not going to work. He rolled out of bed, put his slippers on and went to answer the door. The voices I heard were very faint and I could not hear what they were saying, but I could tell he was speaking to the headmaster. Then they left and went to the headmaster's house next door.

I looked over there. I could see some three or four men and two women sitting on the verandah of the headmaster's house. It looked as if they were quarrelling. I watched as one of the women stood up as if to leave. The headmaster followed her and after what seemed a brief talk, she returned and sat down. I wanted to go and inquire what was taking place, but I thought it was probably none of my business.

After preparing breakfast I sent my neighbour's child to call my husband, but he didn't come. After breakfast I went on with my household chores. I was very worried as well as afraid. Maybe he is in big trouble, I thought. But why doesn't he talk to me? He thinks I'm not a person who is capable of helping. I'll just have to wait and see.

It was late in the afternoon when he came home. I prepared some food which he ate quietly but quickly.

'I saw those people at the headmaster's house. What did they want?' I asked.

'I don't know,'

'How can you say you don't know? You were there all morning and afternoon and I saw you sitting there talking to the people.'

'I hate arguing,' he said. 'Let's have a good afternoon. I want to rest, so please let's not talk about this.' He went straight to bed and after a few minutes was fast asleep.

We were having supper when the headmaster

knocked at the door. I greeted him and showed him to a chair. He made himself comfortable. My husband didn't greet him. This was strange because greeting is always a formality with us. I stared at my husband for some time. He raised his head slowly and our eyes met but then he looked away.

'The headmaster has something to tell you,' he said without looking at me.

My heart missed a beat and then began to pound. I could hear it echo in my ears but I tried to look as calm as possible.

I looked at the headmaster who was now sitting upright and staring upwards as if searching for a microscopic hole in the ceiling. He cleared his throat and then said: 'Your husband asked me to speak to you on his behalf.'

My husband was about to leave the room when the headmaster asked him to sit down. 'If you leave, I am not going to say anying. I told you that I will talk to her,' he pointed at me, 'in your presence.'

Then he looked at me. 'There is a girl who is at my house and there is a case pending. Your husband is involved but there is nothing to worry about at the moment.'

'I-I don't understand.' I said. 'What sort of case? What is this about?'

'Madam,' said the headmaster, 'the girl claims she is pregnant by your husband.' I raised my eyes and looked him straight in his face. I felt like bursting into uncontrollable weeping but determined to keep my cool before these two men. He continued:

'Your husband says he is not responsible for the pregnancy and the girl is going for tests. Let's just all, at this stage, hope for the best.'

'Hope for the best? The best of what? I knew something was wrong. He has not been himself for weeks. He's been drinking heavily, coming home late and not touching his food. He has changed his mind after only twenty-two months of marriage.'

I was about to lose control when I heard our baby stir and got up without a backward glance and went into the bedroom, sat on the bed and started breastfeeding him.

There was complete silence for a couple of minutes in both rooms, then the bedroom door opened slowly and my husband appeared. I looked at him and saw his mouth tremble as he searched for the right words to say.

'I love you and I do care for you and the boy. I want us to stay together. I must have been drunk. I don't remember having anything to do with that girl—I swear I don't. I am not her child's father. Believe me, please. Please do!'

The headmaster must have got up from his chair: 'I want you two to have a good night. No quarrelling,' he said from the next room. 'I will come and see you in the morning.'

With these words he left. I rolled into bed and lay my baby beside me. When I awoke I found my husband asleep on the other side, the baby between us. For the next few nights that is how we slept.

Two weeks later the results of the test from the doctor were out. The girl was not pregnant. My husband paid her parents $300 damages.

I could see the headmaster's house well from where I sat and I saw two women leave the house, one of them carrying a small bag.

I could not believe that any woman would hurt another woman so. Surely women should help one another.

My husband apologised and I forgave him. But I watched those two women until they were well out of sight.

Woman, the Inferior Sex

by Rudo Mufute

Whoever said that
Men have the right minds
Women have the light minds
Was a man of haughty contempt.

When a baby boy is born
They rejoice and ululate
That the family name is retained.
When a baby girl is born
People lower their heads,
For an ill-wind has come.

Why wash clothes
When women are there?
Why cook your own meal
When women are there?
Why worry about a clean home
When women can keep you tidy?

Poor woman, rejoice!
Grab the opportunity
You were an apprentice
But now you are graduating.
Teach the world
That you are fair.

Teach the world
That patterns change.

Young Lady

by Collette Mutangadura

With my head high, I pace the streets
I want a man, a real man
To make a father for the children I bear.
Desperate at heart, I look around.

Some guy whistles. I turn around
But alas, he is not my type.
The guy is not the type of man I want,
The man I have craved for all my youth.

I want that other guy across the street
But he never turns his head
And will never say 'Hi!' to me
Yet it's him I would like to have.

Desperately I look around
For someone I think suitable
To take my hand in marriage
And here I land up with he who offers his love!

Pumpkin Hour

by Lilian Masitera

Little Fanuel falls asleep
While sipping his milk
Invariably.

My husband is seldom hungry
When he hobbles into the house
Benumbed by beer.

This
by the way
happens
every day.

He battles bedwards
Or dares the TV set
To stare him in the face.
They blink each other blind.

Pumpkin hour, at least
Let me rest
And refresh—while my family sleeps
For rise, I must
At six
Tomorrow
And catch a lift
To work.

I undress
And breathe in deeply, relieved
Then I slip into the sheets
Careful
Not to disturb the drunk.

But as sleep engulfs me
Fanuel gurgles from his crib
I rise to check
If he is wet or just awake.

He kicks gleefully at me
I rock him back to sleep
But back in bed
His father is awake
Demanding a fuck.

**Help Fund a
ZWW Rural Workshop
Send your donation to:**

**The Coordinator
Zimbabwe Women Writers
Head Office
78 Kaguvi Street
Harare
Zimbabwe**

Married to Suffer

Anonymous

Every month end my job was to put my signature at the back of the cheque that was my salary—and that would be that. The next thing would be for our letterbox to be flooded with final demands from the different shopkeepers to whom we owed money.

Lazarus, my husband, liked a high class life but was a typical miser. We had been childhood sweethearts and went to the same school although he was two years ahead of me.

Lazarus didn't believe in church weddings—much to my disappointment—as I came from a family where such a wedding was expected. Actually, two of my sisters were nuns and my three brothers had all married in church. Thus, by going to live with Lazarus soon after my training, I became the black sheep of the family.

I was delivered of our first child by caesarian section. Lazarus never came to see me while I was hospitalised for ten days when the incision went septic. He was not at home either, when I was discharged. When he eventually arrived it was to tell me he had been for a job interview and was excited because he'd got the job. There were benefits to be enjoyed by married couples and it was because of this that Lazarus decided we should get married at the District Office. It was a marriage of convenience—although I did not see it that way at the time.

I went back to work exactly four months after the birth of Mabasa, our son. My job entailed travelling. At least for a week every month I would be out of town. We had a car—or should I say, Lazarus owned a car—over which I had no say whatsoever. Teaching me how to drive or sending me to a driving school was out! He believed women who drove cars were all bitches.

He had the same to say about women who dressed in today's fashions and so I was always archaic in my dressing.

If he was in a good mood, he would take me to work. Otherwise the normal thing for me was to walk. I was not allowed to accept lifts from anybody. Because I loved him; because I wanted little Mabasa brought up in a family atmosphere and because I had disgraced my parents, I decided to turn a blind eye to all the injustices. I also strongly believed that divorce was social death.

Many were the nights when Lazarus would stagger home dead drunk late at night. I had orders that I should never ever serve him cold sadza and so I would get up and start cooking fresh sadza for him. Keeping it in the warmer was just not good enough for Lazarus. I had received three or four black eyes in the beginning for trying to defy this order.

What really annoyed me most was that while he sat waiting for his sadza, he would drench himself with urine. Needless to say, it would be my duty to mop it all up and provide him with fresh pyjamas.

When it was time for me to go on my business trips, I'd beg him to give me money, for I never had any. He did the little grocery shopping at the end of each month. All I would get would be two dollars for the whole week to buy things like fruit, cold drinks and biscuits. I remember how embarrassed I would be when I went on these trips with my co-workers. Even the young girls would be loaded with money. I never participated whenever they decided we should contribute to buy something. I would just tell a lie and think of some reason to exempt myself. I was not going to make a fool out of myself. Things like perfume and deodorants I had to do without.

I shall never forget the one occasion when Lazarus assaulted me with an electric cord. I sustained a cut on my left cheek and even today I still bear the scar. I bled so much through my nose and from that cut that I had to be kept in the casualty department overnight.

On that particular day he wasn't drunk. I had arrived late in the afternoon from a trip. I was tired and wanted to go to bed early. Lazarus told the maid who looked after Mabasa, that she was not allowed into our bedroom to clean it. When I went into the bedroom, what I saw was nauseating—to say the least. The room smelled like a gorilla's armpit. There were two soiled sanitary towels on the side of the bed that I normally occupied. It was when I asked Lazarus who the hell it was who had left her filth, that he started assaulting me. He was shouting, accusing me of being a big pretender. He totally denied any knowledge of it. As far as he was concerned, I was so careless and dirty that it must have been me and no one else who had left the mess.

There was now a perpetual state of war in the house. There was serious communication breakdown. Deep inside, I longed for the nights when I would be out on business trips.

One day, in late November, a heavy storm was gathering as we were about to leave work. My colleagues persuaded me to take a lift with them as it was obvious I would be caught in the downpour. I refused at first, knowing what the punishment would be if Lazarus ever discovered it. After much persuasion, however, and after someone suggested they would drop me round the corner, a few metres from our house, I accepted the offer. It had started pouring with rain by then.

They had just dropped me off when a car, at break-neck speed, approached from behind. I had to run for my dear life to avoid being run over. It was no other than Lazarus. For once he had tried to be human. When he saw the storm gathering he had decided to drive me home. He had therefore gone to my place of work and found me gone. Because of the storm, we had all left work early.

Lazarus angrily got out of the car and pushed me into the drain which was fast filling with rainwater. Once again he was panel-beating me, calling me all sorts of names. During the struggle, I slipped and fell on the wet ground, landing on all fours. He grabbed me and tore my maroon overalls to pieces. When he thought he had done me enough damage, he got into his car and drove home. With tears and rain pouring down my cheeks, I followed him half naked. Fortunately nearly all the people were inside their homes taking shelter from the rain.

I went through the evening as if nothing had happened. My face was, of course, swelling up. Lazarus did not say anything more on the matter and I was sure it was all over. Little did I know.

As soon as I got into bed he followed me and started torturing me with a deluge of shouted obscenities. With cigarette stubs he burnt the insides of my thighs. The pain was unbearable. It was the usual accusation— 'Bitch!' By now, Mabasa who had witnessed several of these assaults joined in the screaming. On one or two occasions he, too, had been assaulted.

The following morning when I went to work, my supervisor saw straight away what had happened. She summoned me into her office for a serious talk. On previous occasions she always sent me home whenever I came in with a black eye. She advised me to be firm and stop signing my cheques to my husband for him to squander and entertain his numerous mistresses.

As was usual in the mornings, Lazarus bathed after me. It was while he was in the bathroom that I took the cheque and slipped it into my bag and went off to work. I had hardly settled down when the receptionist phoned to say Lazarus was at reception to see me. I have never been able to describe the feeling I got when I heard this. My heart pounded with fear. I felt a lump in my throat. There was a churning movement in my stomach—something like a hunger pang. For a moment, I could not think straight.

My appearance must have sparked a bonfire in his mind as he demanded the signed cheque. Before I could finish the first sentence his fists were all over me. The fact that there were clients and other staff members present did not deter this barbaric man. Some clients ran away. I heard one person shout *'Hey! Musatiwire!'* ('Hey! Don't fall on us!'). He must have cut my lip with his ring because I started bleeding profusely.

The situation was saved by my supervisor who summoned the company security guard from the gate and also phoned the police.

Once again I had to be admitted to hospital. I had sustained a deep cut on my head that needed seven stitches.

That was enough! My mother came this time when she heard that I was in hospital. She sneaked into our house when Lazarus was at work and took Mabasa and the maid to Chinotimba in Victoria Falls. When I was discharged, I followed them.

I needed to sort out my problems and I took one month's leave from work. My father had already approached lawyers on my behalf. Of course I had long wished to consult a lawyer but I never had any money to do so.

I moved in to stay with a friend until I could find a place of my own. Mabasa had to remain with my parents in Chinotimba. Lazarus had been given orders by my lawyers not to visit or harass me and Mabasa.

Things went smoothly. I had tremendous moral, financial and physical support from my family. I settled into a flat and started my new life as a single parent. Mabasa soon joined me.

One day when Mabasa was coming home from school, he met his father. I don't think Lazarus had much to say to the boy. I never realised how much my son hated his father until the day when he said to me: 'Mama, today I met *that person*'. When I asked which person he meant, he just said, 'The one who used to be my father.'

With that, I got the message loud and clear. I had made the right decision.

In Front of Class

by Hilary Homans

How to maintain interest
remain alert
look alive
in front of class.
Eyes glazed over
Smile fixed on face
I pretended I'm writing notes from the lesson
but really I'm writing a poem—
for Janie—

The fascination of fabrics

Flowing and swirling silk
seductively,
slinking over
lithe and supple limbs.

Denim is a
no-messing-about fabric.
For strength and durability,
For women who wish
to be taken seriously.

Cool, crisp, absorbent cotton,
for freshness
in sticky, sultry summers.

Wool is for warmth
and comfort.
Soft and caressing
for chilled bones.

Hope to Live

by Miriam Gosha

Recuperating in hospital she is
Here and there she looks
With tear-filled eyes
The gods she curses
For being merciless
Only to attempt a smile
When the gentle doctor comes
But hope to live there is

The innocent baby cries
Tired and helpless
It attempts to move
Disturbed soul and sullen face
It attempts to open eyes
Dark and uncaring
The World proves
The young brain searches for thought and question
Where is mummy?
The police come and it's taken
But hope to live there is

Near the graveside
She walks
Memories flood her mind
Good times together
Moments of joy and sadness
Shared success and failure

He is gone forever
A scar left on her life
But hope to live there is

You didn't make it in the exams
The conversation continues
A bit of stammering
A gush of sweat
And a stream of tears
Follow the thought of
What the future holds
And the great let-down to the family as well
A minute's silence
And she faints
But hope to live there is

Starting all over again
She fears
Leaving the children behind
It pains
The occasional fights
Constant quarrels
And periods of anger
Did no good to the innocent ones
And to be touched
Emotional breakdown, yes
It's no longer the same
But hope to live there is

<u>Drought</u>

by Maureen Mataranyika

With it comes all pain and suffering

All poverty and nakedness
The flooding to the city centres
Exploitation of the ordinary man
The dryness both physical and spiritual
The infinity of emptiness
Endless political meetings
Criticism of the Government
False promises
Death and dying
Starvation and sickness
Soaring inflation
Unplanned marriages
Unemployment
Beggars
Street kids
Vendors
Confusion
Mistrust
Crime

My Morning Coffee

by Precity Mabuya

At a quarter-past eight
　　each blessed working day
I get my steaming hot coffee:
　　It will be full to the brim,
Creamish brown in colour
　　Making my mouth water.

My morning coffee
　　You are my hope and inspiration:
Your hotness surges through my body
　　enlivening each and every limb:
You have the glow of a lamp
　　suddenly brought into a dark room.

Sweet, milky cup of coffee,
　　You have a magic effect:
The workload disappears promptly
　　leaving me proud and determined:
Forgetting yesterday's frustrations.

Forward in Time

by Pat Made

I always imagine myself
doing great things
receiving praise
accomplishing some goal

I always imagine myself
surrounded by friends
preaching the 'word'
lavishing in their love

I always imagine myself
better than what I am today
greater than what I was yesterday

I always imagine myself
locked in the past
forward in the future
but away from the present

__Independence__

by the Danhiko School Women's Group

When I got home from the war
I realised our tradition had not changed
we were still second to men
being told what to do

We had to wash
and to cook
and to clean the house
we had to bear a child every year

When I risked my life
during the war
I thought liberation was meant for men and women

Indeed
we got rid of the white oppressor
but today I see we women are still not free

We have to wash
and to cook
and to clean the house
we have to bear a child every year!

But as a person cannot walk with only one leg
this country cannot develop without us!
We are Zimbabwe's other leg
We are needed—oh yes, we are!

Equality—Dignity—and love—Equality!

Choices

by Pat Made

It is now 10 o'clock and I haven't moved an inch from my seat. Ideas. Ideas. A paralysis has gripped my hands and feet. Not one move have I made to my carefully chosen desk to write anything down on paper.

A miasma of hopelessness always engulfs me when I firmly announce to myself and my family, 'Today I want my freedom and space to write.'

Mark, my husband, then prepares the children—Sasha, Sekai and Charlie, also a girl—for an outing so that I can have four to five hours to myself to write.

But I always find myself by the large open window that looks out onto my garden. It is spring now and every colour imaginable peers back at me through the window. I love it here because the beauty and serenity that enfolds me is warm, light and secure.

Looking back at my life—which is now a daily occupation—I see a young black girl with all the advantages: the best schools, college education, a sense of purpose and direction. But somewhere my mind got lost in a melee of wants, desires and comparisons.

I've always wanted to be a writer, but I haven't made any serious attempts at the craft. I've always wanted to be a voracious reader, because any writer of substance will tell you that in order to be a good writer one must read. Can't remember the last time I read a book.

I was sure I'd be a good wife and mother—you know, able to combine my artistic endeavours with creatively rearing three young women and remaining sensuous and fulfilling for Mark. Yet I spend all my time complaining about the lack of space because the girls are in my way. Also, I have to cook, clean, do this, do that ...

Mark never understands. He's made it. A doctorate in his pocket which came from my sacrifices—I even typed the damn paper. He's now a senior lecturer at the University and quite established as an author in his field.

These walls are caving in on me.

Mm...Mm...There's a chill in this room. As I move from my rocker to the kitchen to make a cup of tea, I notice a thunder storm brewing in the distance. Heavy rain pounding on the window always entices me and captivates me in my rocker for hours. I'd better hurry with the tea.

Our house is an old rambling farm surrounded by fields and orchards. We grow vegetables and I preserve peaches, apples and make orange marmalade. But that's the extent of our lives as farmers. Mark and I thought living here would be good for us and the girls. We could preserve a simple way of living and escape the hustle and bustle of the developing urban area. Of course, it means Mark and the girls have a long drive into town for school and work, and I have to do a major shopping trip once a month, but sacrifices are a way of life.

My full-time job, I tell people, is writing. But ever since we left school and the girls were born, my full-time job has taken a new form. I pitter-patter around the house all day and make attempts at keeping the place tidy—we are too principled to have domestic help. Or, I sit in my rocker and recap my life. When it's time to sit down to read or write, I'm too tired or too lethargic. I only come alive again when I notice that it is time to prepare dinner.

The thunder roars nearer as I make my way to the kitchen. I pride myself on this room which is filled with all the kitchen amenities available in the country and decorated with drying herbs and onions, a row of pottery containers on the counter filled with teas, plants, baskets and pictures which depict back-to-basics living and eating.

As I pull my sweater closer around my body and shuffle around gathering all the condiments needed for my special brewed herbal tea, I think what a perfect day for baking bread. Marlet bakes her own bread. Marlet does everything, including working at the University in the agronomy lab. She has a master's in Agronomy and her husband is a post-doc at the University. But then she's quite free—she has no childlren. Oh well, I can't bake bread today, I'm too busy writing.

Mark has suggested too often that I look for a job, 'Maybe journalism, because you studied it in school. It's writing, you know.'

'But it's too defined, too rigid. And besides I wouldn't be able to write what I want to write,' I always remind him. 'Besides, all I need is more time and freedom from my responsibilities.'

'What responsibilities?' Mark asks every time. But, these days, when we go through this same series of discussions, a twinge of annoyance creeps into his controlled voice.

'You, the girls—and everything,' I answer.

"Sauda, I don't understand you,' he says as he moves away to avoid any further discussion.

Well, of course he doesn't understand. He has everything. A knock on the door rescues me from lapsing into another mood of remembering the divide that seems to be growing between Mark and me.

'Hey, Sauda! Let me in before I get soaked.' As I run to open the door for Marlet, I realise the rain has started to pour. Apparently she has been knocking for some time.

'Where were you? Asleep?'

'No, no. I was in the kitchen preparing tea before the rain. But I guess . . . oh well, it doesn't matter. Get in here before we are both struck by lightning.'

'Where's Mark and the girls?'

'Out, so I can write.'

'Are you writing?'

'Just about to get started. But don't worry, I have time for you.'

'Sauda, you have been about to start writing for four years now. I . . .'

'Don't start, Marlet. I'm not in the mood for one of your lectures on women being their own oppressors.'

'OK. What smells like medicine brewing?'

'It's my tea. I'll get a cup for both of us. You go into the sitting room. There's a blanket on the couch if you feel chilled.'

Now alert and ready for the attack, I move swiftly about the kitchen preparing two cups of tea. When I return to the sitting room, Marlet moves away from the bookshelves and falls haphazardly onto the pillows on the couch.

'Thanks,' she says reaching for the mug of tea. "There're some loaves of raisin bread in my bag for you. It's still warm. Get some marmalade and we'll have some with the tea.'

'OK,' I say as I obligingly return to the kitchen for marmalade.

Light peers through a cluster of cumulo-nimbus clouds as I take my place beside Marlet on the couch. The rain is still heavy and I begin to relax as the warmth of the tea flows through my body.

'What brings you out here in the rain?' I finally ask Marlet. We have both been silent for some time, sipping tea, eating bread and watching the rain.

'Wanted to see you, and of course, bring the bread. Can't I come to see a friend?'

'You know what I mean. The last time we talked we got into quite a heated argument about my life,' I said, reminding her of my threat to never speak to her again.

'I know. And I didn't come to start an argument. The bread is a peace offering. Your life is your life.'

'Good, I'm glad you've come to terms with that.'

'How's Mark and the girls? Maybe we can all get together soon.'

217

'They're fine. Mark probably went with them to his sister's place. The girls love it there because auntie never yells like I do. Mark likes it because the food is traditional, good and plentiful.'

'Mm . . . and your cooking still leaves a lot to be desired?'

'I don't have time to slave over a hot stove preparing scrumptuous meals. I'm too busy.'

'Busy writing?' says Marlet sarcastically.

I begin to feel a chill run down my spine as I shift my legs from under me onto the floor. Well, I think to myself, I knew our truce wouldn't last long.

'Sauda,'—the diatribe begins—'you make so many excuses. Yes, I know a family isn't easy for the woman. And I know even "enlightened" men have a long way to go before understanding women's plight. But what about women themselves? What about you? You are your own enemy. Day in and day out you sit hopelessly in that chair of yours thinking about what could be. You've decorated this home the way you think a writer's home should look. You buy the books that you think a writer should read. You dress the way you think a writer should dress. And you even have the gall to announce to people that you *are* a writer. But what have you written? You came here four years ago with Mark and the children—but at that time there were only two children. You had another one to give yourself greater excuses for your own problems. You blame the children. You blame Mark. You even blame me for not having children. What about the women writers whom you admire? Buchi Emecheta has five children. And . . .'

'I'm not them,' I answer softly through my teeth. I can feel the anger burning in my chest and the tears forming behind my eyes. But I know Marlet will not stop and somewhere deep inside of me, I don't want her to stop.

'No one is saying you have to be like them. But stop kidding yourself. Ever since you had the first baby, you've brought your life to an end. Mark told me.'

So she's discussed this with Mark, I think to myself.

'It was as if your world ended with Sasha. Sauda, listen to me. You've been oppressing yourself for a long time. Why punish yourself? It's not too late to put yourself in order.'

'Oh, Marlet,' I begin in a voice which has been subdued by my spirit which has soaked in her every word. She struck a chord when she started to talk about Sasha. 'Yes, part of what you say—maybe everything—is true. What I could be is in my head. What I feel is in my head. Even if I'm not oppressed by those immediately around me. How, dear God, do I break the chains of oppression on my mind?'

'I don't know,' she whispers, now looking painfully into my face which is contorted with confusion.

'I compare myself with you. I compare myself with my friends and the women I knew in college. And always, Marlet, the girl who was voted "most likely to succeed" hasn't succeeded. I have three lovely young women, and Mark is, to all intents, a good man. We are not rich, but far from eating scraps off the streets, I've surrounded myself with everything I want and thought I needed, and still I'm not happy or satisfied. I seem to have fallen far short of my own expectations.'

'We all have, Sauda. No one is perfect and no woman has it all. You've made choices in your life and they may not seem right to you now, but still they were your choices.'

Marlet is closer to me now and I can smell a hint of jasmine. The rain has eased. The drip, drip on the window pane ticks slowly like a clock. I think about her statement on choices and ponder on the idea for a moment. My lips begin to form words and I can feel the weight inside of me pushing them slowly up my throat. I look longingly into her eyes, as if I would find the answer there.

'Were they really my choices, Marlet?'

Were they?

Love

by Rachel Chitsvatsva

The meaning of love continues to elude me.
Perhaps it wasn't there to unearth
But something inside me had to find a reason
To add a touch of value to it.
I had to add tomorrow—to see a future
Though I knew we'd never reach the goal.
Perhaps we just needed, for that moment,
For our bodies to unite
But never our souls.
You have come to haunt me:
Your nakedness I see as open truth
Your freedom mocks me
In this marriage.
I've lost,
grown old
While you still hold your youth.
There is nothing left in me to say
I love you.
We met and shared a moment
Nothing more.

Hitch-Hiker

by Peldah Hove

The bus stop down the road
I found
deserted

Limbs trembling
from fatigue
and fear of the dark
I trudged on
thumbing down
passing cars

The moment I bent back
to heave my bag
from one shoulder
to the other
a car pulled up
by my side.

We travelled in silence
I was captive audience
hosted by cassette
Of the driver's choice.

Thus 'entertained;
we approached my destination
prior to his expectation

for the road to town
still stretched on.

While I found the dollar
for my fare
he thrust a packet
of photographs
onto my lap.

I clutched it, confused
'Mirror, mirror
on the wall . . .'
he moaned
spreading the pictures
of naked women
on the seat
between us.

'Keep your money
Mister woman.
Nothing in his car
costs one dollar
except you, perhaps.
What do you charge
for a fuck?'

I banged his head
with my bag
when he slid his hand
between my thighs
then, bolting from the car
I fled for dear life.

Chains

by Chiramwiwa Lato

I cannot escape
I am bound by chains of wedlock
And chains of tradition are the bolts
No matter how I try
I cannot escape

My house no longer knows love
For it has long gone
Like a flower without water
It has withered

My husband is a stranger
He comes home past midnight
The children fast asleep
His love has become beer

I thank God he does not hit me
But what does that help?
I did not leave my parents home
To come and gaze at his walls.

I came for his love
It is his love I long for.

My mother says 'Persevere.
He will change.'

She pretends she understands
But I know she does not.

One day I will break these chains
One day I will be free
Free from all the false promises
And hope.

What I Saw

by Blessing Chiwona

Strolling in the Communal Lands of Zimbabwe
I saw
a Village
whose crops had been devastated.
Asking poor granny
how she could get along
with the natural disaster
sobs greeted me
before the usual
Handshake.

Strolling in the Communal Lands of Zimbabwe
I saw
Cattle
whose only graze
were tree leaves.
Ribs were countable
walking skeletons
tongues jutting out
awaiting a painful
Death

Ambivalence

by Ruth Mangoma

I was waiting for my younger sister, Farisai, who was supposed to round up the herd which had strayed into the hills. I was the older sister and felt she should obey my orders. She, on the other hand, often acted in a superior manner towards me and made a point of being disobedient. As she came towards me, I felt my anger flare.

Right now it was her turn to fetch water—some four hundred meters away. The hot tropical sun was blazing down on us and I could see mirages reaching into the distance.

'I won't go. And I'm not thirsty,' she laughed provocatively, making herself comfortable on a fallen tree trunk.

'Farisai, please! You must learn to be obedient to your elders—as I'm forever telling you.'

'Oh, you're always giving me pep talks about respect and elders and everything. Our aunt has told me to be free and to do as I please.'

'But you can't expect other people to do everything for you! Now go straight away and round up the cattle and then fetch the water.'

Farisai stared at me insolently. Then she stood up and gave a sarcastic laugh. I was just going to give her a piece of my mind when she spat in my face. Farisai was spoiling for a fight. I stood trembling with anger, trying hard not to lose control. But I could not allow myself to be so insulted. I reached out and slapped her in the face. She had pushed me too far. I hated fighting but if necessary, as every child in the village knew, I could be really rough if the occasion demanded.

All our lives I had been fighting for attention. Our aunt spoiled Farisai and ever since I can remember I have played second fiddle to her. This left me with deep feelings of ambivalence towards my sister—a sort of love/hate—and sometimes I felt a great urge to hurt her. I had that murderous feeling now and thought, either she kills me or I'll kill her.

We struggled, fell, rolled on top of one another and then we got to our feet and boxed. We were fairly equally matched in size and body-weight. She punched my face and head. I fell down and struggled under her, freeing myself. She got hold of me again and bit my ear. I took her by the throat and she gave a tortured cry. I let go. She swerved and steadied herself. Then she sank down and huddled disconsolately against the tree trunk and looked up at me.

We eyed each other, full of hate. Already I did feel a small pang of repentance but I was determined not to show it. I was just about to give her a piece of my mind when, with a look of defeat, Farisai said:

'I'll go and collect the herd, then.'

I was surprised at her easy capitulation. Not for the first time after a scene like this I regretted the episode. I went to the well and sat waiting for Farisai. I took out our packed lunch and set it before me. Though the temptation was hard to resist, because I was hungry, I did not even open it up. I would have done so, but now, after what had happened, I felt guilty and felt I should wait for Farisai.

I swore to myself that I would never again do something so humiliating as fight with her. In future I would not be drawn and provoked into hitting and punching.

For the first time in my life as I sat there waiting, I tried to face the facts squarely. I felt I owed Farisai love. I was 14 when our village was attacked. Our mother, a loving and homely woman was killed as was our father and most of our friends and we were left homeless and parentless. Farisai was only two years old at that time and had never had the benefit of mother love or a family life.

Our village was razed to the ground and Farisai and I were taken to one refugee camp after another. The only close relatives we had were either too poor or unwilling to look after us. Eventually, when Farisai was 7 and I was 19, they found a distant aunt of ours who agreed to take us in. I tried to love her—she was the only real family we had—but she was a hard woman and I was jealous of the way she looked after my sister. She always cared deeply for Farisai and treated me as if I was just around to do the dirty work. It seemed my only function was to fetch and carry and get shouted at. I was now 29, and my little sister was 17 years old.

I was jealous of her. She was pretty and got all the attention in the village. I had always had to look after Farisai's needs: see that she received her share of food, got the best clothes and I had to do most of her work. She was frightened of crowds so I isolated myself with her. She was so used to me being there and doing everything for her that now she looked on me as her slave and if I failed to do what she wanted, she became rude and insolent.

As the years passed, her wants had become more strident. When I tried to wean her from her dependence on me she became impossible.

Now she had been gone for over three hours, looking for the cattle. This afternoon's episode was weighing heavily on my mind. I regretted every moment of it. What was she doing? Where on earth could Farisai be?

I left our food lying on a rock and climbed the hill. I saw some of the herd but no sign of Farisai. I called and shouted times without number and the echoes rolled back from the hills. I tried to beat down my panicky feelings. Where was my sister?

It was going to rain. The clouds, now blackish-grey,

were lowering and the whole sky was darkening. I went further up the hill, calling her name as I went. I penetrated deeper into the long grass. I stumbled and fell on roots and rocks. Once I slipped into a shallow well. I managed to get out but had bruised myself badly. I limped on. Now I was very hungry but the urge to find my one and only sister drove me on.

Anxiously, I thought Farisai must also be hungry but then remembered that she was so fond of *nhacha* that she would sometimes skip meals. The only munhacha tree in the area was on the other side of the river. I retracked back to the river. Large drops of rain started falling. A gust of wind swept a swirl of leaves and there was a tremendous crash of thunder.

I crossed the river. The water was knee deep. And then the rains came down. Twice lightning flashed at me. I was terrified and ducked for cover under a nearby bush. I sat there while the rain sheeted down. The wind was blowing heavily and now and then lightning flared and lit up the surroundings followed by tremendous cracks of thunder.

I sat there for what seemed an eternity and eventually the rain eased to a light shower and then was carried off to the west. A brilliant rainbow formed.

The water in the river was now muddy and foaming. I rose from my kneeling position. My legs were stiff and painful. I limped towards the munhacha tree only to see it had been felled by lightning. For a moment I was petrified by the thought that Farisai might have been struck by lightning—might be lying underneath the fallen tree. But there was no sign of her. I looked for footprints around the area, but there were none.

It was dark now and I was too frightened to go home. I could not face the wrath of my aunt or explain to her what had happened to Farisai. She hated us to fight and had forbidden me to row with my sister. And how could I possibly account for Farisai's disappearance?

I climbed onto a rock on some high ground. If only

I could find my sister! The anger I had felt earlier in the day had vanished. All I felt now was a great sense of love for my little sister. I just wanted her to appear so I could say 'Never mind. I love you'. I wouldn't care if she never ever obeyed me. I thought of all her good points: of her cheerful nature and pretty ways and, after years of feeling she was just an obstacle I was tied to, I realised how much she really meant to me.

Eventually, I fell asleep on the cold, hard rock and in my dreams saw an ugly one-eyed man. He had the familiar aura of my dead father but the face was that of a stranger. He held a large spear in his left hand. He commanded me to come forward and like a fool I did. I knelt at his feet. He laughed. He had two teeth. They were as big as my small finger. I shivered with terror. He made a fire around me. I dared not make any movement or I would get hurt. He placed his spear in the fire long enough to make the head glow red.

'Get up,' he said.

I could not rise because the flames met at a point above my head. It was uncomfortably hot. I wanted to lie down but the fire was too close. He grabbed my arm and dragged me through the fire. I opened my mouth to scream but no sound came.

'Up,' he roared.

I crouched down and clung to his hairy leg, almost like that of an animal. He kicked me off and I went spinning through space, head down into the burning red-hot ashes. And there, in the embers I saw the face of Farisai smiling from beneath me.

I awoke with a loud cry, terrified that the dream was an omen of death. I began to cry. I felt a sense of dread. We had heard of attacks on the hills and perhaps my dream meant that Farisai was dead. With a growing sense of dread, I sat and tried to recall all the details of my dream.

I walked down to the river and checked the depth with a stick. The rain had swelled it, so I swam across.

There was nothing for it. I had to go home. I had to

be prepared to face my aunt and somehow try to account for what had happened. Perhaps the dream was just a warning. I prayed out loud that Farisai would not be dead. Perhaps she had run off to the next village. No one would ever forgive me. I walked along, sobbing as I went.

As I neared the hut, I saw the cheerful sight of smoke coming from the cooking fire. The heavy rain had washed the village into bright raw colours and the early morning grass smelled pungent and delicious.

I hesitated before entering the wire enclosure and then sat down underneath a mopane tree to try to prepare myself for what was to come.

And then, in a rush of relief and wonderment, I saw my little sister Farisai emerge from the hut. She was alive. She was well. She had disobeyed me and run off home.

Sudden angry passion bit at me. I ran towards her and hurled myself at her. 'You rotten disobedient little thing,' I said. I raised my hand and then suddenly I was overcome with relief and remembered how much I'd missed and feared for her.

'I love you,' I said.

ZIMBABWE WOMAN WRITERS

are encouraged to form small writers groups where their work can be read and helpful assistance is readily available. These groups, of 4 to 5 members, usually meet once a week or once a fortnight. They assist writers to unblock, to produce more writing, provide a first-round editing and honing facility and enable writers to bounce ideas around with each other, discussing their proposed plots and themes.
If you are not already a member of a writing group, FORM ONE NOW.

Fate of the Mongoose

by Anita van der Heiden

(In 1967, just before her 10th birthday, Anita fell off the back of a municiapl lorry and was unconscious for many months. When she regained consciousness, she found she was blind and unable to speak or walk and had limited use of her hands. Anita can type and read braille and also manages to use an electric wheelchair. She is a prolific writer.)

There's a chicken on the lawn
What a noise it makes
It's been sitting there since dawn
The ground around it quakes.

Perhaps it's just hatched a chick
Do let's go and see
Come on Hendry, don't be thick,
This chicken's not a she!

Oh my goodness! Oh my crumbs!
A mongoose on the run.
I'm all fingers, but no thumbs.
Quick Hendry, get your gun!

Hendry wasted not a sec
Out of the house he strode.
Shot the mongoose through its neck
And flung it on the road.

Side by Side with You

by Colette Matangadura

I buried myself and rose up anew
My womanly scream I buried too
I brushed away my frightened thoughts
To fight side by side with you.

When you took up arms ready to fight
(The enemy only understood the gun)
I stood beside you. The shots rang out
I was by your side, my brothers.

Through thick forests I combed the land
Vigilant of the enemy
If my gun fired second to yours
Well, that was that for the Motherland.

I will always fight side by side with you
And put away the womanly things
I will march abreast with you
And fire the gun of liberation.

Who has liberated us, you or me?
Who has fought two wars, you or me?
The first to brave my womanly fears
The second which liberated us all.

I buried myself and rose up anew
The gun was frightful for a woman to see—
To see it laying about unused.
I took it up and fought the war.

The Emancipator

by Nyaradzo Makamure

I know her.
A sweet language—
Diverse—
Like the world's cultures;
The Emancipator

Colour her
Black
White
Yellow or
Red,
She will remain
The Emancipator

Carved out of Zimbabwe's heritage
Endowed with natural rhythms,
Her hug, all embracing.
She is the Emancipator.

Lose her through cunning,
Sweet talk
Indoctrination
Propaganda
Fun, frolic and frivolity
But she will always be
The Emancipator.

Win her by
Solidarity of purpose
Strength in Sisterhood.
Perpetuate gains made through the
Strength of motherhood.

The choice is yours, but
Bear the consequences.
It is yourself to blame
If you have deserted
Your Emancipator.

My emancipator?
Of course, I know her—
The Vote!

UNSAFE ISSUES

Debate and discussion on these issues
is encouraged
by Zimbabwe Women Writers.
The revelations of women's experiences are
sometimes held back because of fear of job loss,
implication and even imprisonment of self or of a
family member, and generally retribution by
society.
A major workshop on Unsafe Issues revealed
the main areas of unsafe issues:
Rape
Child Abuse
Sexual Harassment
Unwanted Pregnancy
Abortion
Wife and Child Battering
Birth Control
Baby Dumping
Sexist Attitudes and Practices

Mother

by Egely Donadi

Mother
On the hard, sunbaked earth you toil
On the infertile soil you scratch
Barren land—since time immemorial
Which bears no fruit

With no rain
No clouds in the sky
The sun burning hot
You try to restore life into the dusty soil

With nothing in your stomach
Or on your cracked feet
With bruised and worn hands
You wrestle with nature

Your sweat waters the infertile soil
Your tears water the unproductive earth
You labour, unpaid,
Day in, day out

You are the worker of the day—
Of the week—
Of the month—
Even of the year

Mother!
You are the best worker in the world

Unsafe Issues

by Norma Kitson

(Written for the ZWW First Public Reading at the National Gallery, Harare, in February 1990 , following the Unsafe Issues Workshop led by Amanda Hammar, and performed as the finale by the cast of ZWW following comments by various men on the Workshop)

Forget the unsafe issues—
The clitoris is hidden.
PMT is just your lot,
The menopause, God-bidden.

Prostitutes are bad for men,
And what's more they wear trousers.
Rapists are provoked by girls—
Their tits show through their blouses.

Forget the unsafe issues—
Menstruation is unclean.
Pregnancy's God-given
And AIDs is not my scene.

I don't like wearing condoms
Its just like sex in socks,
Can't help it if its dangerous
And I give you the pox.

Forget the unsafe issues—
And please forget debate.
I don't like women meeting,
Its something that I hate.

Just be a normal woman
And pray to God above.
You may well hold up half the sky
But you are just my love.

(And incidentally, while you can,
Just earn a bob or two.
And while you're at it, darling,
A couple of kids will do.

And mother's not too well today
And brother's socks need sewing
And will you fetch the water?
And remember - there's the hoeing.)

Forget the unsafe issues—
Lesbians just need a screw.
Housework's right and fitting.
Motherhood's natural too.

Abortion's very wicked.
Birth is mere mechanics.
Please forget about HRT—
Don't play with your organics.

**Debate the unsafe issues!
Down with the terrible lies!
More power to Zim Women Writers!
As we hold up our share of the skies.**

**And remember, while you're at it,
That women do most of the grind.
We'll shove off the yoke of oppression,
To the benefit of all humankind.**

Not a Picnic for Mom

by Barbara Makhalisa

She had not meant to eavesdrop. She'd only come to gently break the bad news. Her right hand was folded into a fist, knuckle of forefinger ready to knock on the door when her daughter's loud voice froze her to attention as she heard Nobuntu say:

'I don't care what you say. Mama is mean!'

'She's not, Buntu!' said Langa in his cool manner.

Nomasonto visualised him stretched out on his back, trying to concentrate on his latest adventure story borrowed from the township library, and only half paying attention to his sister.

'She is!' Buntu insisted. 'Dad is more fun!'

'He's not!' Langa protested, impatience creeping into his voice.

'Well, he is! Who usually takes us out to fun places? And when did we last eat ice-cream in this house? We only get it when Dad takes us out.' At that Nomasonto let out an involuntary 'Oh!' and did not realise that her forehead was knit into a pattern of ridges.

'You can't live on ice-cream, silly goat!'

'Yes I can.' Buntu's voice was shrill. "I could have ice-cream for breakfast, lunch and supper—every day! Not the veggies Mama forces us to eat.'

'That's not fair, Buntu. Mama gives us good food.'

'Good food? My foot! Sadza, sadza, every day! And those horrible veggies. "Eat them, they're good for you." I say they aren't good for me. I want ice-cream and chocolate and chips and fizzies. Daddy always gets us those.'

'Our teacher says that's junk food. And don't you talk like that 'cos Mama cares for us.'

'Cares? Ugh! "Polish your shoes! Pick up those clothes! Don't play—do your homework first! Blah-blah-blah!" Dad never shouts at us.'

'I bet he would if we lived with him.'

'Never! Dad always buys us what we want and takes us where we want to go.'

Nomasonto could see her indomitable daughter in her mind's eye with her big challenging eyes glaring at Langa. She was never one to be outstmarted in an argument, whether she was right or wrong. Nomasonto could also tell that by now Langa had sat up on his bed, determined to squash this pest.

'But he does not want to live with you. Has he ever taken you to his home?' Buntu was quiet for a while. Then she said wistfully, 'Wish he would.'

'Well, he doesn't want to! He left Mama for that other woman. He lives with his other children. He does not really care for you.'

Nomasonto felt her heart palpitating. She had heard enough. Hands on her beating heart, she shuffled to her room and dropped onto her bed in tears.

My God! she thought. Oh my God! She had never imagined how her seven-year-old felt about her. It's not fair, she thought. This is what I get for struggling to give them everything so they don't feel out of place with their friends. She tried to tell herself that she should keep calm in order to quieten her crazy heart-beats, but she was too full of unexpressed resentment .

Her estranged husband was one of the top executives in his company. Look at that car he drives, and the house he lives in, she thought to herself. And what a struggle it was to get money out of him for the children's upkeep. At times she could not sleep at night trying to figure out ways of making him contribute towards the children's support. She had done enough arguing with him before he walked out on them. Little good that had done her!

He did not love her any more he said. Those words still stabbed at her heart. He had gone on to say she was a mistake in his life.

'But I love my children and I'm going to take care of them.'

But then he had other children to take care of. He became too busy to spare much time for these children. Nomasonto had pleaded for her children's sake, but he was brutal.

'Stop hiding behind the children and face reality, will you,' he said as he went out with some of his clothes draped over his arm. That was how they had disappeared from the wardrobe in dribs and drabs. She'd begged him to stay—to no avail. She felt helpless and unwanted.

It was humiliating. She pictured her neighbours and friends laughing at her and gossiping. She lost her appetite and did not care how she dressed or how she looked. She became so depressed she almost lost her job. It took her kind boss talking to her to make her realise her children would suffer a double blow if she lost her job.

She determined to work hard for her children. She was not going to let them become ping pong balls wrangling with him. Eventually they settled into a routine where he fetched them once a fortnight and took them out. The children looked forward to those visits with their father and she hated to see the longing in their eyes when they came home and he turned his back and drove off after each visit.

On this day he had just phoned to say he could not fetch them—an emergency had come up. And now she had overheard these sentiments from her children! She felt deflated.

She was not actually sure what she wanted. If he did not come to take the childrten out, she fumed with bitterness and resentment. So, he didn't care! He had his other children day in, day out. Couldn't he spare just an afternoon every two weeks to be with these children? Hadn't he fathered them? Was he not the one who had given them the names Langa and Nobuntu? Once he had called her his lovely sunshine. And he had always said her personality outshone all others. Where had she gone wrong? And when he did take them out, she felt abandoned and angry.

It was not fair to cancel this appointment. Didn't he know she needed a break too? When he did come to take the children out, she usually managed a smile and waved them goodbye for the afternoon. But inwardly she fumed. It was just not fair. He was just a picnic Dad while she had to do all the donkey work. The children were always in a good mood when he came to fetch them, but she had to contend with their sulks and tempers.

'I'm a person, not a piece of wood,' she hissed aloud, holding her head. Why could she not be a picnic Mom? Then she would not spend every cent on buying food and clothing, rent and transport. She could also give them special treats.

Earlier she had planned to make herself an omelette and a cup of tea for lunch. But now that there were two miserable faces to think of, she had to plan something special. 'Sadza, sadza, every day!' 'When did we last have ice-cream in this house?' Buntu's words bit deep. Well, there was no way she would be forced to eat a morsel of sadza this afternoon.

She did not have much in her savings account. And in her 'Rainy Day' savings bottle she did not have much more than forty dollars—which she had been saving to get Buntu's hair plaited in that lovely style she always looked at so longingly on other girls. Well, she could save for that again. The priority now was to do something to appease the explosive situation after announcing the bad news.

She stood up and emptied the bottle onto her bed and began to count. Ten, twenty, twenty-five, thirty, thirty-seven, forty-six dollars and ninety-four cents. Thirty-six dollars would go towards lunch. Four dollars for ice-creams while they played at the park. Oh yes, today she would be extra patient and let them have their fill at the swings, the see-saw, the slide and the jungle jim. Then they would linger at the bubbling brook and the fish pond. After four hours of outing, they would be tired enough and ready to go back home. Maybe Buntu would not be so bitter and resentful after that.

She stood up and walked back to the children's room and knocked at the door. They were both quiet and preoccupied. Two pairs of eyes turned to her with curiosity and expectation. Nomasonto smiled. She actually looked forward to the day out with her children. It would be Buntu's special outing.

This is the first attempt by Zimbabwe Women Writers to write, typeset and publish a full-scale book. Please give us feed-back and let us know what you think of the content and production. Our Shona & Ndebele Anthology is planned for 1994/1995.

UnderBlock 46

by L.Humphrey

Beauty wormed out carefully from under the corrugated iron sheeting. With a quiet movement she pushed the sheets down so that the entrance to UnderBlock 46 remained undetected. As she squatted in the yellow light cradling the bottle she heard the Geriatric guards squirming back down the tunnel from which she had just emerged. Their old, whining voices were still rinsing her ears with their complaints.

 —He's going to die, anyway. Just like the rest of you.

 —Your brother, isn't he?

 —You young ones are nothing but trouble. Sick all the time, messing everywhere. Work, work, work. That's all we do for you. Then we have to risk our lives organising burials for you when you die. Can't trust anyone these days, least of all Body-Packers.

 Now, above ground, in the distance to her right, she saw the rats. Like the dogs and crows, these mutated creatures lived off the land—or what was left of it. The ultraviolet sun rays and toxic water seemed to have no adverse effect on them. They hunted in packs, carried weapons and often formed alliances with the Organ-Hunters. She knew she could not outrun them, but she could outwit them. They had not spotted her yet, so, taking advantage of the poor light, she wedged herself between two dead trees. The rats walked past her in animated conversation with one another. They were discussing the departure of the final flight to the Megaconglomerate.

The Megaconglomerate had long been using Zimbabwe as a dumping ground for its waste and, in return, members of the tribe of High Ones were allowed free access to its goods and services. But from now on, they too were stuck here with the Geriatrics and the Neophytes. The Megaconglomerate had terminated contact because the levels of toxins in the air had affected the aerocraft's take-off ability. Some toxins had even been transported back to the Megaconglomerate causing unidentifiable illnesses—illnesses which for years had been decimating the working pouplation of Zimbabwe, leaving only the old and the young alive, but barely living.

The girl had no time to think about the significance of the rats' conversation. Her immediate task was much more important. She had to find clean water for her brother. For days now he had been unable to drink the laboratory-manufactured liquid supplied to UnderBlock 46 by Unit Control. Clean water was as unobtainable as fresh, unpolluted air. There was water around, but drinking it or touching it was fatal.

Washing or bathing, of course, was prohibited and everyone in the UnderBlocks took tablets to deaden their olfactory senses.

The girl had seen her brother's condition before— with the HIW virus that had killed their mother two years ago. Suddenly the image of his small, shrunken body with its sunken eyes flashed before her. For weeks now she had watched helpelssly as he lost his strength. Not that any of them had ever had much strength. Living in their cramped boxes underground, breathing constantly recycled air and eating artificially-processed food, most of the inhabitants of the UnderBlocks survived only a few years longer than those who lived AboveBlock. The UnderBlocks were a last refuge for the Geriatrics and the Neophytes. Almost all Parentials were dead: killed by years of exposure to carbon monoxide fumes and other poisons, deadly rays of the sun and HIW. The UnderBlocks were havens for those who were considered valuable by the High Ones. The others—the street kids, the homeless, the unemployed—had nothing with which to buy themselves a place. They were deemed dispensable and roamed the AboveBlocks, a constant threat to the UnderBlocks.

She turned in a north-easterly direction, thinking of her brother. If he didn't have water soon, he wouldn't last 24 hours. She was his only hope. She hoped that the well her grandmother had spoken of really existed. In her last days she had rambled endlessly—and it had been impossible for the girl to decide what was fact and what fantasy. Her grandmother had spoken of the sun rising in the east and sweeping the sky in a kaleidoscope of colours. The green of grass in summer, the brown in winter, the white of the summer clouds and the blue of the winter sky Beauty had seen only in photographs. She could not imagine that trees once stood upright, their proud leaf-clad branches reaching into the blueness above them, their trunks, cylindrical and strong, thrusting myriads of roots into the earth.

Her grandmother's stories had been mind-gripping, all about life before The Drop. Then, the movement of the sun determined time—and daytime had been light and night-time dark Beauty hated the monotonous, clammy yellow that enveloped everything now. How she wished that she had paid even more attention to her grandmother—perhaps then she would know exactly how far it was to the Kopje. The distance would have remained the same, even though everything else had changed. She walked gingerly, avoiding any sodden ground which, caving in, would land her in an Organ-Hunter's trap. Her eyes had become accustomed to the dank yellowness and she stretched her neck forward as she walked. Her ears throbbed from the effort of listening. There seemed to be no one AboveBlock, which wasn't all that surprising as only yesterday the Patrol had warned of a radical increase in toxic levels. The

Geriatric and Neophyte scientists, without the benefit of the knowledge of the 1990/2000s Parentials, could not make up their minds about what caused these levels to rise or fall.

The sounds of wild barking and snarling came to her and in the shadowy gloom she could pick out the shapes of four dogs. They had something cornered and were taking turns to dive and snap at their victim. Beauty could see feathers flying into the air and she was close enough to hear the flapping of wings. The dogs had surrounded a crow—an unusual feat, as they generally stayed well out of reach, screaming and cawing from the mounds of rubble that used to be the houses, schools, clinics and office buildings of the city. The dogs stood on their hind legs and thrashed at the crow with their front legs. Their eyes glinted greedily in anticipation of their meal. With claws extended, teeth bared and muscles stretched, they inflicted as many wounds on each other as on the crow. In a desperate swoop, only just skimming their heads, the crow flew off, having taken advantage of a small gap between two of the dogs. They yelped, turning in circles to give chase, and dashed down the very path that Beauty had followed ever so carefully minutes before. Suddenly there was quiet. Beauty crept out from behind the wall. The dogs had vanished. She heard a muddy gurgling noise to her left and located the spot just in time to see a dog disappearing as quickly as an ant into an ant-lion's trap. The Organ-Hunters, none too fussy whether their victims were dead or alive, would already be freezing the dogs and checking their data bases for customers. Dogs inner ears were highly prized and, for those with the money or the connections, a transplant could easily be arranged.

Beauty stood, riveted, staring at the innocuous-looking muddy patch. She knew full well that she had missed the same fate only by a whisper. She estimated that she had about another kilometre to go, but three Transversals to cross. The Transversals separated Blocks

247

and delineated areas of command. Although being AboveBlock was dangerous enough, at least she had the permission if not the protection of the Block Commander. Getting permission to leave the Block had not been easy. It was out of respect for her mother that the Commander had finally given in to Beauty's request to leave the block. Before she had fallen ill, her mother had been a valued scientist. She had invented the Brain-Trans Ray which enabled the High Ones to collect and store the combined knowledge and wisdom of the Parentials. Soon after The Drop, that historic day on which it was collectively decided that life above ground was no longer possible, the High Ones and the scientists had a meeting. It was agreed that any Parentials wanting protection for their families in the UnderBlocks after they had died would undergo a Brain-Trans. That way, all human knowledge in Zimbabwe could be collected. Beauty's mother was responsible for this programme. Unfortu-nately, she had died before she perfected the method of passing on the collective know-ledge to the Neophytes. This meant the loss of thousands of human years of knowledge and wisdom. The education of the Neophytes was now in the hands of the Geriatrics whose knowledge was outdated and sometimes even dangerously wrong.

Beauty was approaching Ardbennie, the first Trans-versal. She peered around, trying to locate the Transversal Alarm. An elaborate network of gigantic eyes, mirrors and sonic beams was used to guard the transversal perimeters and the only way to by-pass this was to wait for a buzz car. Buzz cars, arriving and departing from Unit Control at unspecified times, deactivated whatever section of the Transversal they were travelling along. There was a second Transversal, Remembrance, to be crossed about 100 metres further up Ardbennie. Beauty decided that a buzz car, either turning left, from Ardbennie into Remembrance, or right, from Remembrance into Ardbennie, would deactivate both Transversals at the same time and provide her with an opportunity to cross both. She pressed herself into the shadows, crossing her fingers for luck. This, so far, had been good and seemed set that way. Within a few moments she heard the whooshing sound of an approaching buzz car. In less time than it takes to blink, the car had turned from Ardbennie into Remembrance. Beauty, bending low, ran diagonally across the two Transversals. She had succeeded! Elated, she scaled the four-foot wall that separated the cemetery from the Transversal. The next part was easy—the cemetery was unguarded and, except for the Body-Packers, was generally avoided by the AboveBlocks. Beauty had only to walk to the furthest end of the cemetery and cross the final Transversal, Rotten Row, to reach the Kopje. Years of living UnderBlock, however, had weakened her muscles. She felt them trembling with exhaustion. Her ankles and knees failed to support her and she had no choice but to squat for a time with her back against the wall.

In front of her were rows and rows of signposts. Years before it had been decided that graves should be vertical and, as stones took up too much space, each grave was marked with a signpost, standing about three foot high. As graves were shared by family members, each signpost had several names. Beauty wondered where her grandparents and parents were buried. Visiting graves was strictly forbidden and whenever someone in the UnderBlocks died the Geriatric guards contacted the Body-Packers who buried the person in the family coffin. She shivered. She turned her mind to a more pleasant subject and one that never ceased to fascinate her—life before The Drop. Back then, death was but a small part of life, the full stop at the end of a meaningful, eventful existence. AboveBlock, in those days, was alive with people, walking, cycling, laughing and talking. No one lived underground then except some animals and low-life forms like worms and snakes. Now life underground, in the UnderBlocks, was a living death. The demographers had predicted that within 20 years Zimbabwe would be de-peopled. Even the far away Megaconglomerate, seemingly protected with all its sophisticated technology and wealth, had a bleak future.

Beauty lifted herself up. She had left her brother an hour ago and had permission to be away for two hours only. The graves stretched endlessly ahead, the signposts as close together as bristles on a brush, and the only way to make quick progress through to the other side was to walk next to the walls, along the perimeter. Ten minutes later she saw the Kopje looming up ahead. She realised that not all her grandmother's ramblings were crazy. She had said that few knew of the well on the Kopje's northern side and that it was unguarded. Beauty waited for a buzz car and made it across the last Transversal in the same manner as before. She decided that she would try to hide herself in a buzz car on the way back. But for the moment she had to try to remember where the well was located.

The Kopje was bigger than she had anticipated. Closing her eyes in an effort to remember her words, she tried to recall her grandmother's gentle voice. Through the mists of memories she heard it. She felt slightly dizzy and sank to the ground.

—The well, ah, sweetest water. Next to the biggest mango tree I ever saw.

—A mango tree? What's a mango tree?

—A fruit tree, my darling. With big yellow fruit. Orange flesh that melts in your mouth.

—And, you could pick your food straight off a tree?

—Straight off, dear heart. Or pull it from the earth.

Beauty shook herself and moved her thickened tongue in her mouth. The mango tree would lead her to the well.

She couldn't recognise a mango tree, but she could look for a huge tree, now dead, of course. She began her search. It didn't take long. After a few minutes she saw an enormous tree on its side. It must have taken long to die and it was still covered in blackened leaves. Tortured, ignoble death. Next to the tree stood the well, an old-fashioned one, similar to pictures she had seen in her mother's girlhood storybooks. She drew up the bucket—

it was full of holes. She had expected to less. She attached her bottle to the rope and, with mounting excitement, lowered it. She heard the bottle filling up with water and when the gurgling stopped, she pulled it up. It was full. The water was clear and sparkling. Not like the milky white liquid they drank UnderBlock. And certainly not like the black sludge that lay in puddles AboveBlock. Joy filled her soul. So, this was water. Like a miser with gold she sprinkled some drops into her cupped palm. The drops merged. With delight she saw the lines of her hand magnified; she saw minute bubbles of water twinkling inside the bigger bubble, air trapped between her skin and the water. She lifted her hand to her mouth and licked her palm. She opened and closed her mouth, pursing her lips in an effort to recognise its taste. A look of bewilderment spread over her features. Could it be this that would save her brother?

　　With a shock she realised that she had less than half an hour in which to get back. The Commander disliked having to use extra guards at the UnderBlock exit when someone insisted on going AboveBlock. Retracing her steps to the Rotten Row Transversal, she thought she may as well try her plan and hide in a buzz car. She saw one turning left from the Robert Mugabe Transversal. Luck was with her—it was a big, slow one, garbage-powered, and unpopular with the High Ones. With no difficulty at all she stepped inside and slid down between the seats to hide. Buzz cars had no drivers, and she fervently hoped that the radiation warnings would mean that the High Ones would stay safely tucked away indoors. She slipped the bottle out of her radiation repellent vest in order to sit more comfortably and as she did so she heard the nasal voices of High Ones. They spotted her just as she was trying to squirm down further between the seats.

　　—What have we here?

　　—A Neophyte UnderBlocker, by the looks of it.

　　—Who are you and what do you think you are doing AboveBlock?

The girl stared at them with popping eyes and opened and closed her mouth, noiselessly. Her main concern was that they should not see the bottle of water.

The buzz car was making its way along the Transversals and she could see the Ardbennie Transversal ahead. With every ounce of strength in her body she threw herself between the High Ones and right out of the buzz car. She hoped that they were not wearing their radiation repellent vests and that they would think better than to follow her. There was no one behind her. She had now only two blocks to cover beore reaching UnderBlock 46. The water was heavier than she expected and slowed her down. For once she was thankful for the yellow mist that filled the AboveBlock streets and the mounds of rubble that lay everywhere. The entrance to UnderBlock 46 was well disguised but she recognised it by the corrugated iron sheeting. As she left two hours previously, so she returned. The Geriatric guards were still on duty.

—Made it, did you?

—Didn't expect to see you again!

She chose to ignore them and went straight home to her brother. His condition was the same but he smiled weakly when he saw her with the water. She smiled back lovingly and on the piece of paper she put in his hand he saw the words:

Real water. Drink.